Understanding Architectural Drawings

A Guide for Non-Architects

John J. Cullinane, AIA

The Preservation Press
National Trust for Historic Preservation

The Preservation Press
National Trust for Historic Preservation
1785 Massachusetts Avenue, N.W.
Washington, D.C. 20036

The National Trust for Historic Preservation is the only private, nonprofit organization chartered by
Congress to encourage public participation in the preservation of sites, buildings, and objects significant
in American history and culture. The National Trust carries out this mission by fostering an appreciation
of the diverse character and meaning of our American cultural heritage and by preserving and revitalizing
the livability of our communities by leading the nation in saving America's historic environments.

Support for the National Trust is provided by membership dues, contributions, and a matching grant from
the National Park Service, U. S. Department of the Interior, under provisions of the National Historic
Preservation Act of 1966. The opinions expressed here do not necessarily reflect the views or policies of the
Interior Department.

Printed in the United States of America
97 96 95 94 93 5 4 3 2 1

Library of Congress Cataloging in Publication Data

Cullinane, John J., 1942-
    Understanding architectural drawings : a guide for non-architects
        John J. Cullinane.
        p. cm..
    Includes bibliographical references.
    ISBN 0-89133-202-2
    1. Mechanical drawing. 2. Buildings--Specifications
    3. Construction contracts. I. Title.
    T353.C95 1993
    692' .1--dc20   93-22079

Designed and composed by John J. Cullinane, AIA
Printed by the Baker-Webster Printing Company, Washington, D. C., on recycled paper

Understanding Architectural Drawings

Contents

Welcome to *Understanding Architectural Drawings*. This book was written as a guide for "non-architects," that is, individuals not specifically trained, through education or experience, in reading and interpreting contract and construction documents.

Although architects and engineers make valiant efforts to communicate their design ideas and construction techniques clearly to anyone who may be reading their plans and specifications, the fact is that a lexicon of architecture has evolved over the years that can inhibit such attempts. This lexicon, the language of architecture (and engineering), is represented on drawings by symbols, signs, words, and abbreviations that can defy interpretation by the novice. Although this notation and vocabulary may not be as confusing as Leonardo da Vinci's upside down and backward writing, for the uninformed understanding it can be like trying to read a totally unfamiliar language.

This book has been created to assist individuals who may be responsible for reviewing drawings and evaluating construction documents, or who just have that interest. *Understanding Architectural Drawings* is designed to demystify drawings and specifications, to reveal the inside tricks that are practiced by every architect, and to provide the tools necessary to understand drawings and how they are created.

Understanding Architectural Drawings is divided into sections illustrating various components of contract and construction document development, with the greatest emphasis being placed on drawings and specifications. There is a large section on the "Language of Architecture," basically an illustrated dictionary, for reference, and recommendations for further reading and reference material. The book is, logically, graphic based. And to the extent possible, the illustrations, symbols, notes, and drawings are shown as they would normally appear in a set of construction documents.

As you might imagine, there are many more elements to a set of documents than could be included in this one volume and many elements that can only be learned through years of practical experience. However, *Understanding Architectural Drawings* will provide the user with enough information to understand drawings and specifications and to avoid feeling inadequate when confronted with design and construction questions, or a pushy architect.

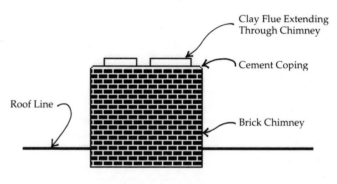

Chimney Flue

A number of elements comprise the documents used to construct a building or structure. Most of these are important to architects, contractors, owners, and lawyers.

When looking at a full set of documents for a construction project, you can view it as being like one of those wooden dolls which, when opened, is found to contain another doll, and then another, and another, and so on. Similarly, the large number of components that make up a set of documents contribute to the full package.

The full package would be referred to as the "contract documents." These include everything from the contract forms between the owner and contractor to change orders executed during construction. This is the set which is the basis for the construction contract.

A subset within the contract documents would be the "bid documents." These include the forms to be used by contractors when submitting prices for construction, the plans and specifications for the project, and any addenda (changes) to those plans and specifications issued prior to submission of construction bids.

Within the bid documents are the "construction documents." These are made up of final plans and specifications, addenda, bid alternates that were accepted by the owner, change orders as they are developed, and shop drawings as they are submitted and approved. When reviewing documents for a project, the components that are most important are, of course, the final plans and specifications, the additive or deductive alternates included in the bid documents, and any change orders executed as the project progresses.

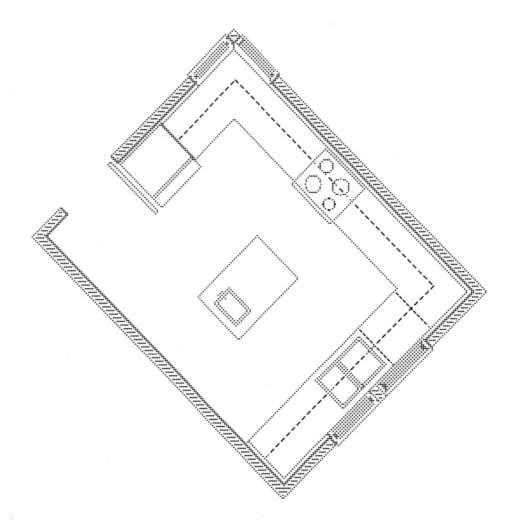

By the time a set of construction documents has been produced for a project, whether it is new construction or rehabilitation of an existing building or site, a number of stages of work have been completed leading up to that point, and quite a few more will be required before the project is completed. Each of these stages influences the final design and treatment of a building and site.

Development of a project is a linear process, with each step requiring reviews and approvals before the next step or stage can be undertaken. In most cases, even before the architect or engineer is involved, the owner has made some basic decisions regarding site location, building use, and budget. In some situations the owner may even have started developing a building program.

Once the architect is commissioned, the first step taken on most projects is to initiate or complete program development. In this stage of a project, the potential users identify their needs and how they would like the structure or site to function. The initial requirement -- identification of needs -- will be very specific. It will include such things as specifying the functions that will be performed in the building or on the site, how many people will use the facility, what equipment will be used or required, and anything else that could influence the size or design of the project. The second element-- how they would like the building or site to function-- will usually be very general. It may include things like whether the owner wants the project to function as a catalyst for revitalization of a community, whether it should serve as a corporate or personal symbol, or what their image of the design may be.

In addition, a building program will identify the zoning and building restrictions and standards that will govern or impact the final design.

Once the program is accepted the architect will develop a "concept" or "schematic" design. This will establish the basic form and size of the structure and its location on the site. In the cases where there are more than one potential site, additional concept or schematic designs will be developed.

This is the first point at which there will be a major design review. The drawings and illustrations presented by the architect at this stage will generally be in rough-sketch form and show the interrelationship of spaces and functions through diagrams and charts. If there are questions regarding site selection, they would be resolved prior to approval of the concept design.

After acceptance of the concept, the architect will move on to the "preliminary" design. During this process the program requirements and approved concept will be developed and refined into something that looks like a structure or building. The actual form and overall dimension will emerge, the approximate location and size of openings will be noted, and the proportions of rooms will be established. Where the structural engineer would have been consulted in development of the concept design to decide the basic building material, in the preliminary design stage all of the consulting engineers-- civil, structural, mechanical, electrical, fire-safety, and, if appropriate, acoustic--will be made part of the design team. In addition, a landscape architect and interior designer will be consulted.

The next stage is development of the "final" design. Here is where the final building and site material will be selected and the color of brick, stone, and species of wood chosen, as well as such things as the types of light and plumbing fixtures. At this point, probably the most critical review takes place. The owner has spent a minimum amount of money to this stage, and changes in the design will be easier now than when the project progresses. This is when a lot of projects are submitted for review to local, state, and federal agencies. The presentation drawings developed by the architect to show his final design are geared to sell the project. Accordingly, they are usually considered ideal for submission to review boards and agencies.

Acceptance of the final design leads into development of working drawings and specifications. Within architecture and engineering offices, the first step in this process is undertaking "design development." This is the stage of work where all of the elements and factors leading up to and including the final design are analyzed, synthesized, homogenized, pasteurized, and made to work. Working as a team, all of the architects and engineers figure out how to create a puzzle of parts that, when properly assembled, will result in a structure or site that looks like the final design and functions in a manner that meets the owner's program requirements. The design development on a project starts at the point that the final design is approved and continues through completion of working drawings.

The result of all of this effort will be a set of bid documents--drawings and specifications. At times this will be the point at which a project is submitted for review. At this stage of the work, changes to the design are both time consuming and expensive. At the preliminary and final design stages any changes can be relatively easily incorporated into the design development; but once the drawings and specifications are completed, changes affect all aspects of the project. This could require redesign not only of the building, but also of the structural, mechanical, and electrical systems. The only prudent reviews at this point are those that ensure that the drawings and specifications properly reflect the approved final design and program requirements. In other words, reviews now would be more technical than design in nature.

The next few stages come in relatively rapid succession:

Bidding. Drawings and specifications are sent out to contractors for prices. (While the bidding process is under way, any changes to the drawings or specs are referred to as addenda.) The bidding process will usually take from three to six weeks, depending on the size and complexity of the project.

Opening Bids and Contract Award. The bid forms in the package provided to contractors will specify a location, date, and time for the delivery and opening of construction bids. This is a process normally open to the public, at which most of the general contractors interested in doing the work will be present. Once the competitive bids are opened, the owner and architect will review the cost proposals, comparing overall prices, and the bids for any add or delete alternates that may have been included in the bid package. (Add alternates are items that the architect or owner really wanted but were afraid would cost too much, and delete alternatives are items that the architect and owner could live without if the overall construction price comes in too high.) The owner will then choose what is considered the "best bid." This may or may not be the "low bid," that is, the least expensive proposal. In some cases, the best bid may be presented by a contractor who has unique experience or ability, making that person the best one to undertake the work even though he or she may not be the least expensive. The process of reviewing bids and awarding a construction contract will usually take between 30 and 90 days.

Construction Start-up. Normally, the successful bidder will be required to obtain all building permits and start construction within a week or two of receiving a "notice to proceed." At this point the primary responsibility for the project shifts from the architect to the general contractor (GC). A number of things happen simultaneously at this stage. The GC notifies all of his subcontractors, providing each with a schedule of construction activities and delivery dates for their materials. Each subcontractor then places the necessary orders for material and equipment in order to meet the schedule requirements. In addition, material and equipment manufacturers will start development of "shop drawings" for submission to the architect and engineers for review and approval. During the process of construction, the architect acts as an agent of the owner, reviewing construction activities and quality of the work. Any modifications to the drawings or specifications during the construction period are referred to as "change orders" and are incorporated as part of the final contract documents.

At the completion of construction, the architect and engineers will review the work in detail and develop a "punch list." This is a complete listing of all additional work or corrections that have to be made to meet the contract requirements. Once the additional work is complete, the project is turned over to the owner to occupy. There, a simple process.

As you can see, there are a number of stages at which program and design changes can be accomplished, and a number of points where reviews are necessary. These include the preliminary and final design reviews and the evaluation of the bid package for addenda and alternates that could change the design of the project and that affect existing resources. (It is not uncommon for the bid package to call for one type of material to be used, such as wood windows, and also an alternate of lesser quality. In such a case, acceptance of the alternate, which will usually be based solely on price, could change the character and quality of the project.) Reviews are also useful at the bid-evaluation stage and when change orders are made during construction.

Although there is no industry standard for the size or format of architectural or related drawing sheets, or for the scale of the drawings themselves, within a single set they will almost always be consistent. Generally, the drawing-sheet size will be the largest that is practical. This is often determined by the size of the building itself, the size of the equipment used by the architect, and the paper stock available. Often preprinted drawing sheets are purchased and used on as many projects as possible. In most cases the sheet size will be 24" x 36" or 30" x 42". When a particular project will not easily fit on this size, custom sheets will be either handmade or printed. Drawings that are too large to be practical for carrying around on a project site will usually be reduced 50 percent.

There is some consistency, however, in the way a drawing sheet is laid out. After many years of experimentation, most architects and engineers have found that information regarding the drawing itself is best located on the far right-hand side of the sheet. This allows an individual easy access to drawing numbers and titles without having to open the entire set. The drawing information can appear clustered in the lower right-hand corner, or it may extend up the entire right side of the sheet. The architecture or engineering firm, the original drawing date and dates of any revisions, sheet numbers, and sometimes drawing scales are all identified.

If the entire drawing is one scale, rather than many drawings at different scales, it will be shown in this box.

The Date block will normally contain the date on which the drawing was originally printed.

The Revisions block will list dates on which revisions were made to the drawing. This ensures that a reader knows which version of the drawing is currently being viewed.

The name of the architect or engineer of record, that is--the individual or group responsible for the design, will be shown on each drawing.

The name of the project and/or owner will appear on each drawing.

The Drawing block will show the name of the drawing, such as "First Floor Plan."

Large plans will often have a "Key Plan" located in the drawings. The shaded area will indicate that portion of the building shown on that sheet.

The Sheet # block will show the drawing series, such as architectural, structural, or landscaping, and the sheet number in that series.

Key Plan

Scale

Date

Revisions

John Cullinane Associates
Architects & Preservation Planners
Washington, DC

Louisville School of Art
Anchorage, Kentucky

Drawing

Sheet #

A-6

All of the floor plans, whether architectural, structural, mechanical, or electrical, will be drawn at the same scale. In other words, if the architectural floor plans are drawn at 1/4" = 1'-0", then all of the corresponding engineering floor plans will be at that same scale. This ensures consistency in reading the drawings and makes life a lot easier for the contractor. As drawings progress from complex to simple--floor plans to building details--so the scales of drawings will progress from small to large, for example, a floor plan drawn at 1/8" = 1'-0" and details drawn at 3" = 1'-0". The scale of each image is usually noted just below the title of the drawing. In the case where the set of drawings may be reduced, a graphic scale is used, rather than a written scale. As the metric system comes into more-common use in American architecture, double scales and dimensions will appear on drawings, one English and the other metric.

A set of drawings is filled with various symbols which act as a sort of shorthand for the architect and engineers. These range from simple north arrows, showing the orientation of the structures, to symbols for structural connections and electrical, mechanical, and plumbing fixtures. Each profession has its unique set of symbols and icons. In addition, the context in which certain words will be used will have special meaning. Even common words, such as "do" and "equal" take on new significance when they appear on construction plans. To assist the viewer and contractor in reading the drawings, the set will normally include a number of "legends" defining the symbols and icons. In most cases, however, the indications are common enough that they are familiar to those who are required to use them.

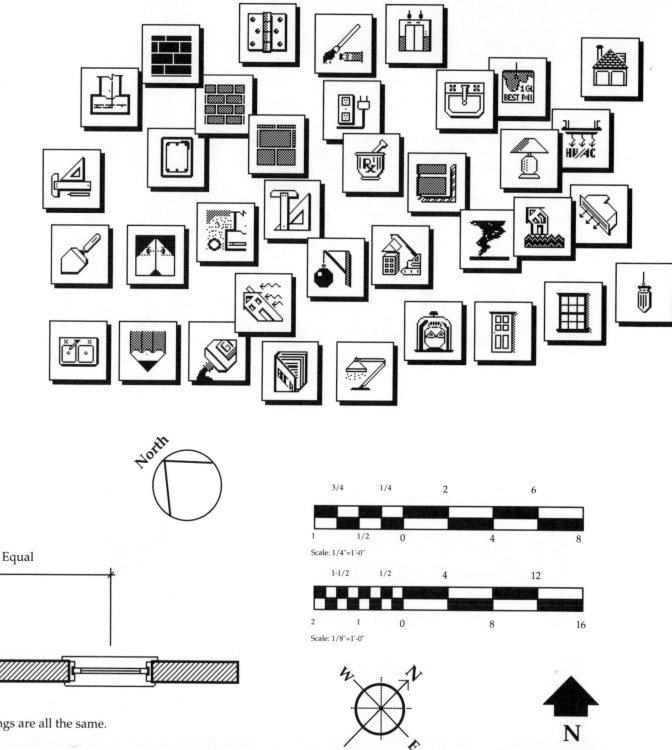

North

3/4   1/4   2   6
1   1/2   0   4   8
Scale: 1/4"=1'-0"

1-1/2   1/2   4   12
2   1   0   8   16
Scale: 1/8"=1'-0"

Equal   Equal

The word "equal" means that the dimensions or spacings are all the same.

W N
S E
N

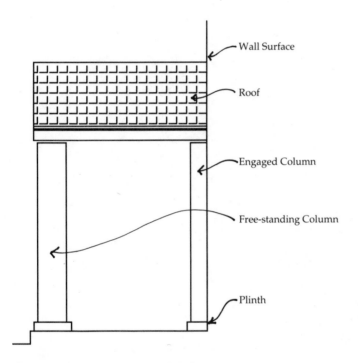

Labels on diagram: Wall Surface, Roof, Engaged Column, Free-standing Column, Plinth

Free-standing and Engaged Columns

Drawings are the primary means of communication for architects and engineers. They are the tools used to instruct and direct contractors on how to assemble a building or structure. Drawings illustrate the materials and systems that, once placed in the pattern and form shown on the drawings, will result in a building designed to meet specific program needs.

You will find the term "drawing" used in two different ways. One is a reference to the sheet of paper or film on which an image is drawn. The other is the image itself. In this chapter, the term "drawing" refers to the image on a sheet of paper.

The size, form, and type of a drawing is generally dictated by the size of the building or detail being depicted. However, some conventions and standards have developed over the years. There is always an attempt to make the drawing as large as practical. The larger the image, the more detail can be shown, and fewer unknowns will be left to be worked out while the building is under construction. Drawings are almost always drawn in scales that allow a contractor to use a standard tape measure to determine actual dimensions. Because tape measures are usually read in feet and inches, these are the units of measure used on drawings. Also, because tapes are divided into sixteenths of an inch, and most easily read in one-quarter-inch units, most drawings will be in increments of that unit, such as 1/16" = 1'-0", 1/8" = 1'-0", 1/4" = 1'-0", 1/2" = 1'-0", and 3/4" = 1'-0". It is unusual to see a drawing in an odd scale, such as 3/8" or 5/8".

There can be one or more images on a drawing sheet, and a number of drawing sheets constitute a set of drawings. This set may be referred to as construction drawings or working drawings; both terms mean the same. A set of drawings, in turn, generally will be divided into sections related to different types of work. A typical set for a moderate-size project would include the following:

Cover Sheet. This would include information on the name and location of the project, the owner, architect, engineers, and other consultants. In addition, the cover sheet might include an index to the drawings in the set.

Site Plan. Site plans would be indicated by the letters "SD" (site development), followed by the sheet number for each sheet that illustrates work on the project site. Site-plan sheets would include surveys of the site, topographical elevations of the earth and buildings, any changes in grades or ground contours, plus locations for drainage on the site. In addition, most site construction, such as paved areas and sidewalks and fencing, would be shown in this section of the set.

Landscape Plan. This is indicated by the letter "L" preceding a sheet number. The landscape drawings show existing and new plantings, and special site lighting and furniture. These drawings would also usually include a schedule (list and number) of plants and planting materials, and any irrigation system on the site.

Demolition Plan (D). When there is substantial demolition as part of the project development, one or more demolition drawings will be necessary. These will simply show what elements should be removed from the site or from any existing building or structure.

Architectural (A). This will usually be the largest portion of the set of drawings. All of the general new construction will be shown on these drawings. Within the architectural section of the set, convention has dictated that there be a subset, proceeding from the smaller-scale overall image to the large-scale detail. The section will usually start off with floor plans and move to building sections, elevations, enlarged floor plans, wall sections, interior elevations, finish schedules, door and window schedules and details, and construction details. There will almost always be variations to this subset, depending on the type of building, the type and extent of drawings required to convey the design and method of construction, and the amount of time the architect devotes to the set of drawings (the more time, the more drawings).

Structural (S). The structural drawings for a project will most often be developed around the architectural floor plans. These will show floor and roof framing patterns, structural members, and details. Depending on the complexity of the project, there may be beam schedules showing the size, configuration, and reinforcement of each structural member. When the project involves an existing structure that will be rehabilitated or expanded, these drawings will indicate which existing structural members should be changed or improved, plus the addition of new members. On projects of any size, i.e., larger than a single-family house, structural design and the accompanying drawings will be done by a licensed structural engineer. On small projects an architect will risk doing the structural design.

Mechanical (M). The mechanical drawings illustrate all of the heating, ventilating, and air-conditioning systems for the building and will include piping and ductwork details and often plumbing. Like the structural drawings, they are generally based on the architectural floor plans. (In fact, on many projects the structural, mechanical, and electrical engineers simply use halftone reproductions of the architectural floor plans on which to draw their systems. When this is done, the plan of the building appears as a gray image in the background, while the engineering drawing shows up as dark lines in the foreground.)

Electrical (E). The electrical drawings in a set show all of the wiring and outlets in a building, and the electrical service to the structure, and will include a schedule of lighting fixtures. There will also be an electrical riser diagram in most sets, as well as illustrations of any special light-installation details.

Plumbing (P). Although the architectural drawings consistently show the location and type of plumbing fixtures, such as water closets and sinks, the plumbing drawings provide all of the hot and cold water piping, wasteline, and vent locations. In addition, this section will include plumbing riser diagrams and schedules of fixtures.

Fire-Safety (FS). Depending on the size of the project, there may be a separate fire-safety set of drawings, or the locations and types of smoke and fire detectors could be shown on the mechanical drawings.

In addition to those listed above, a set of drawings may include other groupings of drawings, such as Interiors (I) and Acoustics (AC), which follow the same pattern of using the architectural floor plans as a base drawing and overlaying it with data.

Illustrated on the following pages are a typical site plan, floor plans and elevations, building sections and wall sections, some interior elevations and details, and schedules. These drawings include dimensions and notations as they most typically appear in a set of working drawings. Notes referring to the meaning of a symbol or notation are located in the shadow boxes.

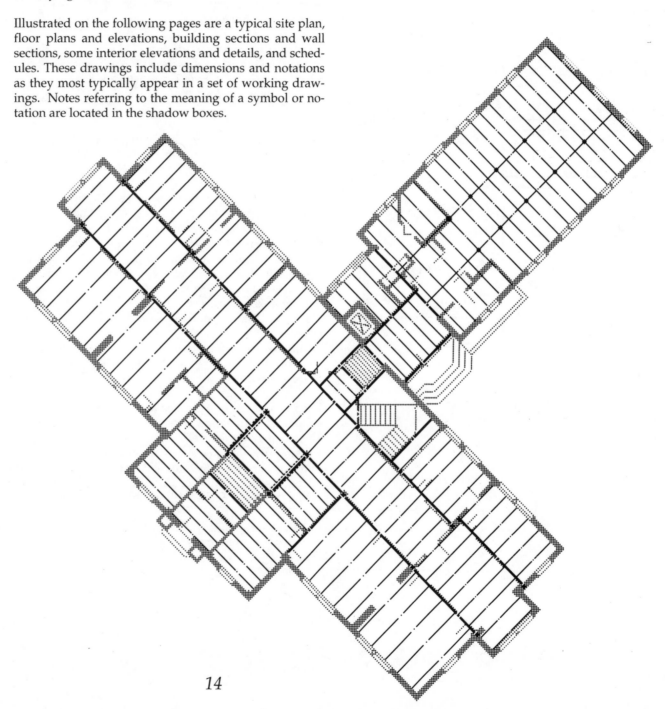

In the set of drawings the site plan is the first description of the project in the set of drawings. It will illustrate the limits or boundaries of the project and all of the general aspects of the site and its condition. Generally, the site plan will be a topographical survey done by a surveyor, with existing and new buildings or site improvements superimposed on the plan. The survey will include all of the information required by the contractor to place a structure on the site, such as electrical service location, sewer hookups, and special elements. Of greatest importance on the site plan will be the location, both vertically and horizontally, of any site improvements. In the case of a new building, the horizontal distance of that structure from at least two property lines, or other site elements, will be indicated. In addition, all vertical elevations will be indicated in relation to what is called a "benchmark." This benchmark may be an official elevation marker anchored in a sidewalk, on a concrete post, or on another building. Most often, though, the benchmark reference will be something much more informal, such as a nail in a tree, or a wood stake driven into the ground with a nail in it, or an "X" marked on a piece of pavement on or close to the site. Just about anything will work, just so it is stable. An official benchmark plate will indicate its true elevation above sea level, while an unofficial benchmark will be given an arbitrary elevation, usually 100'. Everything is then measured from that point. So the site plan may indicate that the first floor of the building is at elevation 101.5', meaning that it will be 1.5' above the height of the benchmark. The basement elevation on the same structure may be shown at 86.5', meaning that it would be 13.5' below the height of the benchmark. All vertical locations for structures or site elements will be in relation to the benchmark.

The site-development plan will also show existing trees and other elements that would affect construction. There would be indications of any existing constrictions, such as underground tanks or remnants of old structures, and notations of any special actions the contractor should take before initiating work.

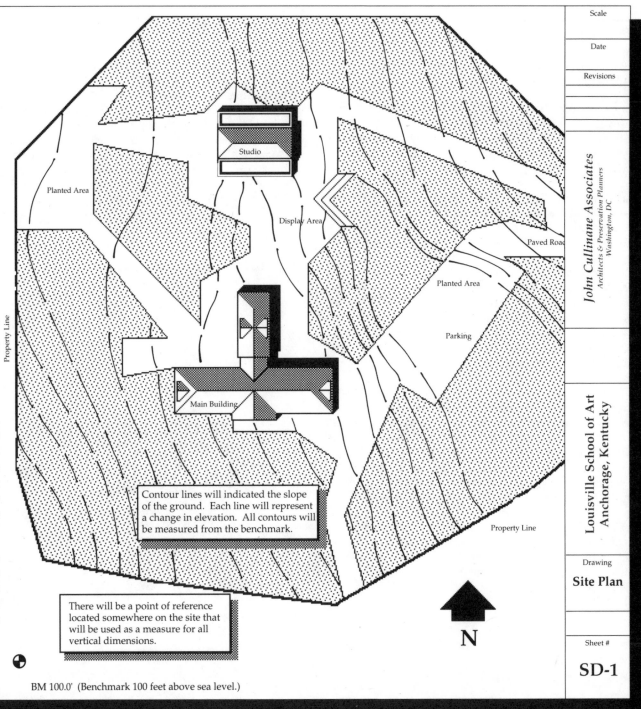

Scale

Date

Revisions

John Cullinane Associates
Architects & Preservation Planners
Washington, DC

Louisville School of Art
Anchorage, Kentucky

Drawing

Site Plan

Sheet #

SD-1

Studio

Planted Area

Display Area

Paved Road

Planted Area

Parking

Property Line

Property Line

Main Building

Contour lines will indicated the slope of the ground. Each line will represent a change in elevation. All contours will be measured from the benchmark.

There will be a point of reference located somewhere on the site that will be used as a measure for all vertical dimensions.

N

BM 100.0' (Benchmark 100 feet above sea level.)

Landscape plans and specifications can be some of the more confusing components of a project. This is partially due to the fact that landscape architects themselves have a professional language, most of which is in Latin. We may look at a particular tree and think "Holly." They look at the same tree and say "Ilex aquifolium." Same tree, but their name is a bit more precise.

A landscape plan will be one of the first drawings in the set. It will generally be identified with the prefix "L," and will illustrate the topography of the site and existing and new plant materials. In addition, this plan may include site lighting, furniture, and irrigation systems.

Using a halftone of the site survey as a base, the landscape drawings usually incorporate information on what existing plantings should be removed or moved and show patterns of new work. This may include earth moving, which will have been illustrated on the site plan. The plan itself is an aerial view of the site from somewhere above the top of the tallest tree. In almost all cases, the drawings depict the trees without leaves, but show the existing or anticipated reach of their branches. Bushes and shrubs are shown as outlines of their full shape. Flowers and ground cover are usually indicated by dots, indicating their planting pattern and location.

In addition to showing the plants and trees, each landscape element is identified either by a direct notation or by a number or letter that refers to a "Landscape Schedule." This schedule provides the Latin name for the plant, its size (in pot size or diameter), the quantity of that particular plant, and any special planting instructions. Also, the landscape drawings generally show some typical planting techniques to ensure proper installation.

The landscape drawings are the only ones that consistently provide the contractor with the quantity of material, such as a number of specific plants. All other drawings require the contractor to estimate or calculate the amount.

A long time ago, when architects were more draftspeople than computer operators, plants and trees on landscape drawings were rendered by hand. Architects took care to illustrate the correct branch pattern and shape for each species, creating, in some cases, works of art. As technology advanced, rubber stamps were made showing different types of plantings. Possibly because of the ease of use of these stamps, it sometimes appeared that more landscaping was indicated around buildings than with earlier, hand-drawn plans. Time and science marched on, and the rub-on, or transfer-tree, came on the market. This provided the architect with a very clean, sharp-lined image of a tree, available in both plan view and elevation. Current technology now allows the architect to superimpose computer images of trees on the site plan, all taken from vast libraries of computer clip-art.

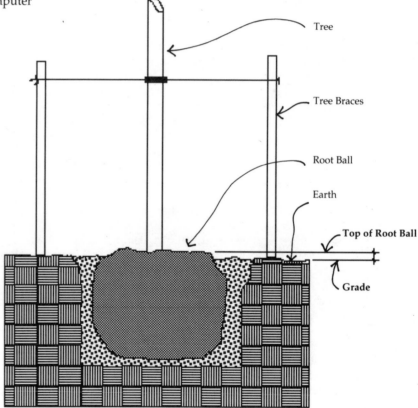

Tree Planting Guide

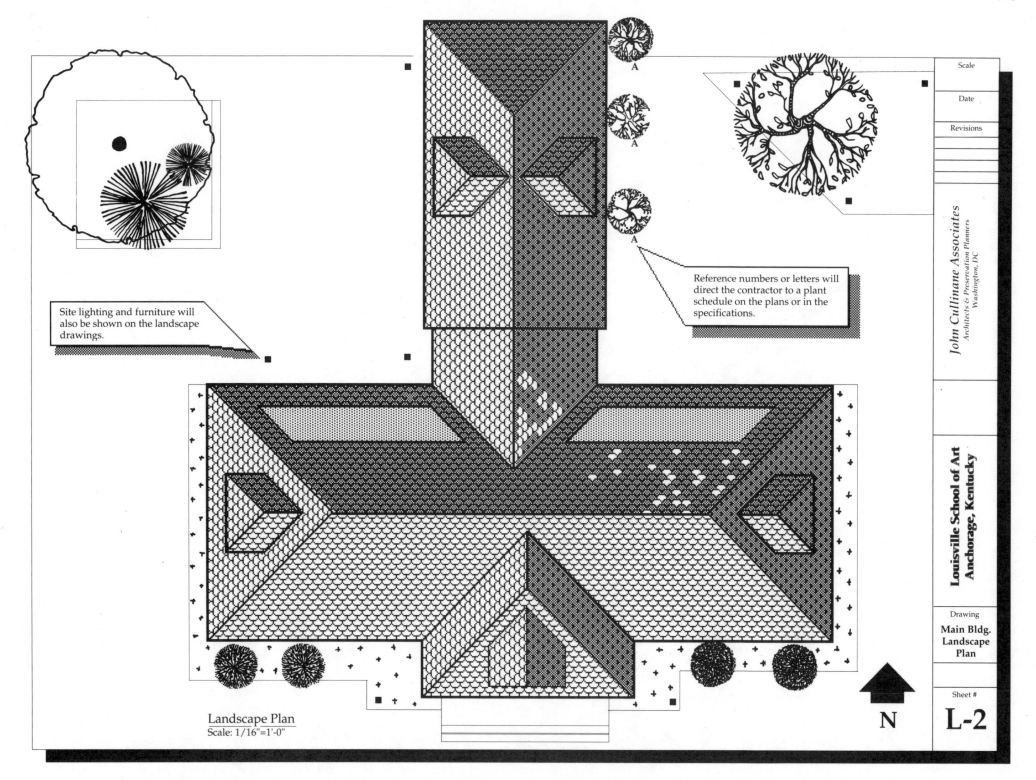

Site lighting and furniture will also be shown on the landscape drawings.

Reference numbers or letters will direct the contractor to a plant schedule on the plans or in the specifications.

A

A

A

Landscape Plan
Scale: 1/16"=1'-0"

Scale

Date

Revisions

John Cullinane Associates
Architects & Preservation Planners
Washington, DC

Louisville School of Art
Anchorage, Kentucky

Drawing

**Main Bldg.
Landscape
Plan**

Sheet #

L-2

N

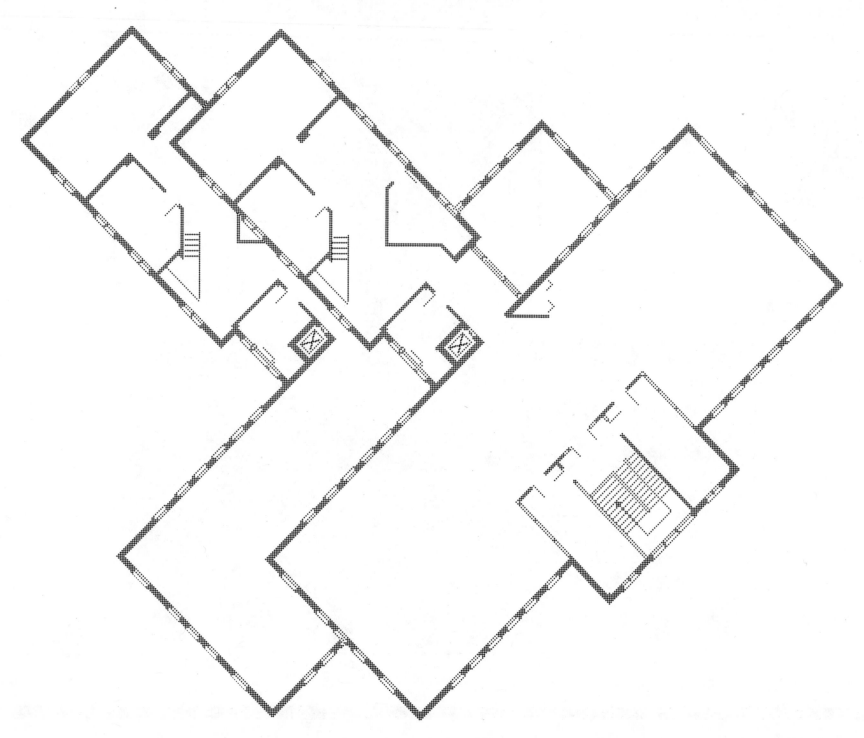

Floor plans are the central, critical element in a set of architectural drawings, providing the contractor and reviewer with essential information on building configuration, dimensions, interior spaces, circulation, and materials. Floor plans also serve as a basic index to building components, such as windows, doors, and finishes. Within a set there may be numerous groupings, starting with the overall plan of the building drawn in a relatively small scale--1/16", 1/8" or 1/4"--followed by enlarged plans of areas of particular complexity. Each level of a building or structure will normally have its own floor plan. In some cases where the building may have many floors with the same configuration, such as in high-rise office buildings, there may be a "typical floor" plan in the set. In these situations the typical plan tells the contractor that a certain number of floors will all be laid out the same. Otherwise, there will be separate plans for each floor. Within the set, these start with a plan of the lowest level of the building first and progress up through the structure.

The large floor plans in a set of drawings will give an overall understanding of the building, and a tremendous amount of information essential to the work to be done. Each space or room is identified with a number, letter, or combination of both, which will appear on these drawings. These designations are linked to room finishes materials, colors, equipment, and fixtures, such as lights. In addition, the large floor plans provide an identification for each door and window opening, linking them to size and design schedules elsewhere within the set. There will also be references to enlarged floor plans, building sections, wall sections, and details.

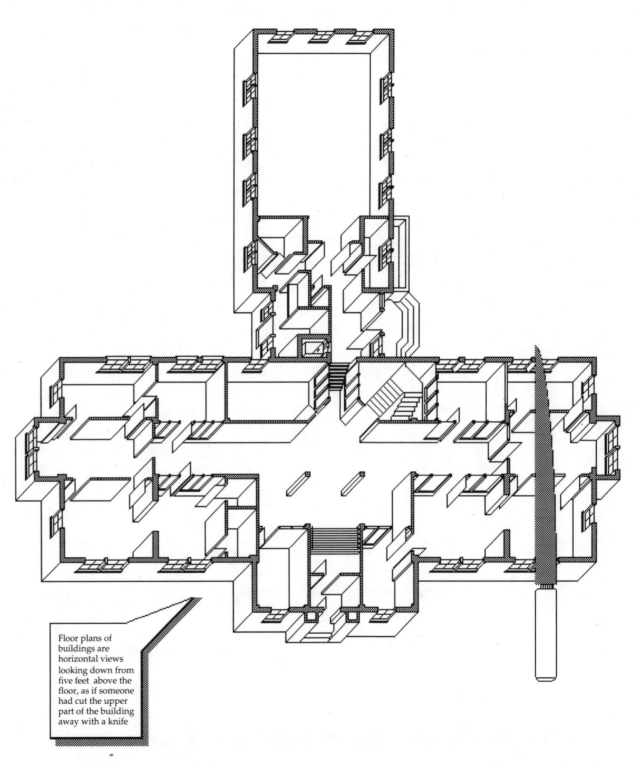

Floor plans of buildings are horizontal views looking down from five feet above the floor, as if someone had cut the upper part of the building away with a knife

19

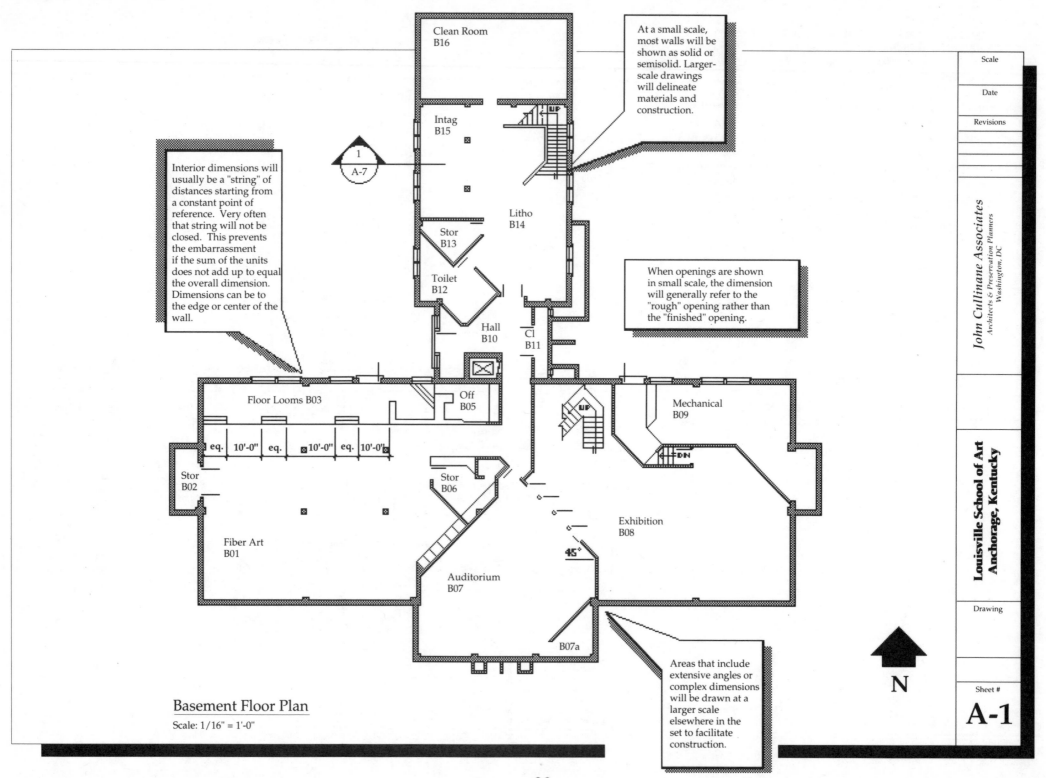

Clean Room
B16

At a small scale, most walls will be shown as solid or semisolid. Larger-scale drawings will delineate materials and construction.

Intag
B15

1
A-7

Interior dimensions will usually be a "string" of distances starting from a constant point of reference. Very often that string will not be closed. This prevents the embarrassment if the sum of the units does not add up to equal the overall dimension. Dimensions can be to the edge or center of the wall.

Litho
B14

Stor
B13

When openings are shown in small scale, the dimension will generally refer to the "rough" opening rather than the "finished" opening.

Toilet
B12

Hall
B10

Cl
B11

Floor Looms B03

Off
B05

Mechanical
B09

eq. | 10'-0" | eq. | 10'-0" | eq. | 10'-0'

Stor
B02

Stor
B06

Exhibition
B08

Fiber Art
B01

45°

Auditorium
B07

B07a

Areas that include extensive angles or complex dimensions will be drawn at a larger scale elsewhere in the set to facilitate construction.

Basement Floor Plan

Scale: 1/16" = 1'-0"

N

John Cullinane Associates
Architects & Preservation Planners
Washington, DC

Scale

Date

Revisions

Louisville School of Art
Anchorage, Kentucky

Drawing

Sheet #

A-1

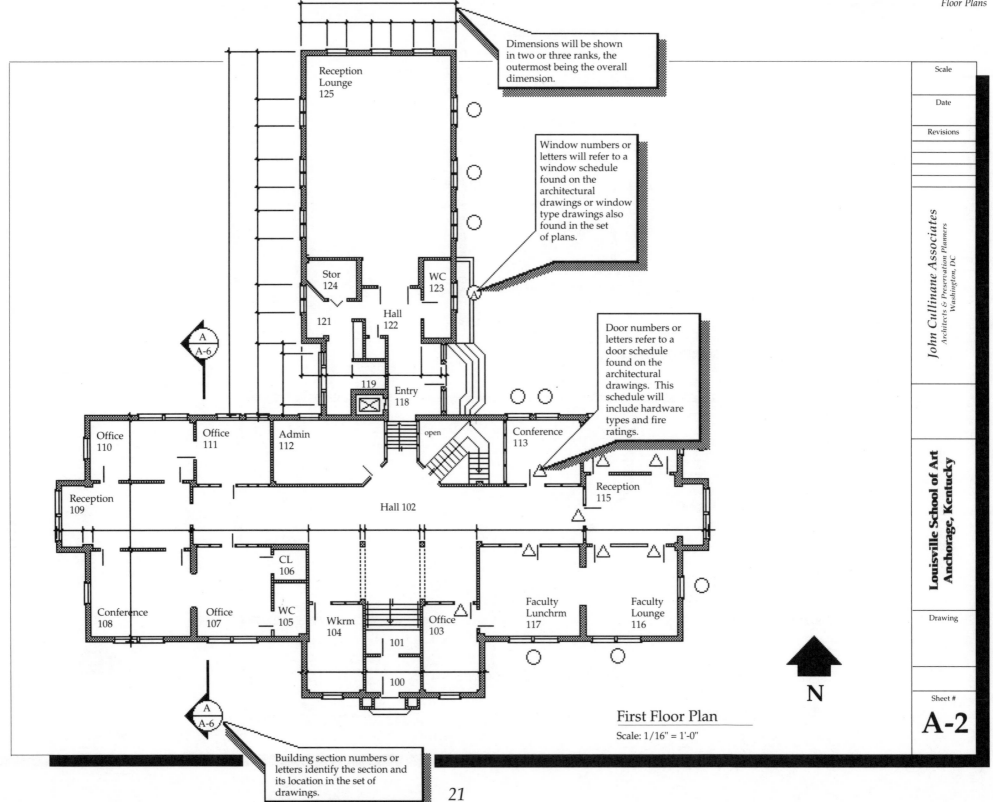

Dimensions will be shown in two or three ranks, the outermost being the overall dimension.

Reception
Lounge
125

Window numbers or letters will refer to a window schedule found on the architectural drawings or window type drawings also found in the set of plans.

Stor
124

WC
123

121

Hall
122

Door numbers or letters refer to a door schedule found on the architectural drawings. This schedule will include hardware types and fire ratings.

A
A-6

119

Entry
118

Office
110

Office
111

Admin
112

open

Conference
113

Reception
109

Hall 102

Reception
115

CL
106

Conference
108

Office
107

WC
105

Wkrm
104

Office
103

Faculty
Lunchrm
117

Faculty
Lounge
116

101

100

Building section numbers or letters identify the section and its location in the set of drawings.

A
A-6

N

First Floor Plan

Scale: 1/16" = 1'-0"

Scale

Date

Revisions

John Cullinane Associates
Architects & Preservation Planners
Washington, DC

Louisville School of Art
Anchorage, Kentucky

Drawing

Sheet #

A-2

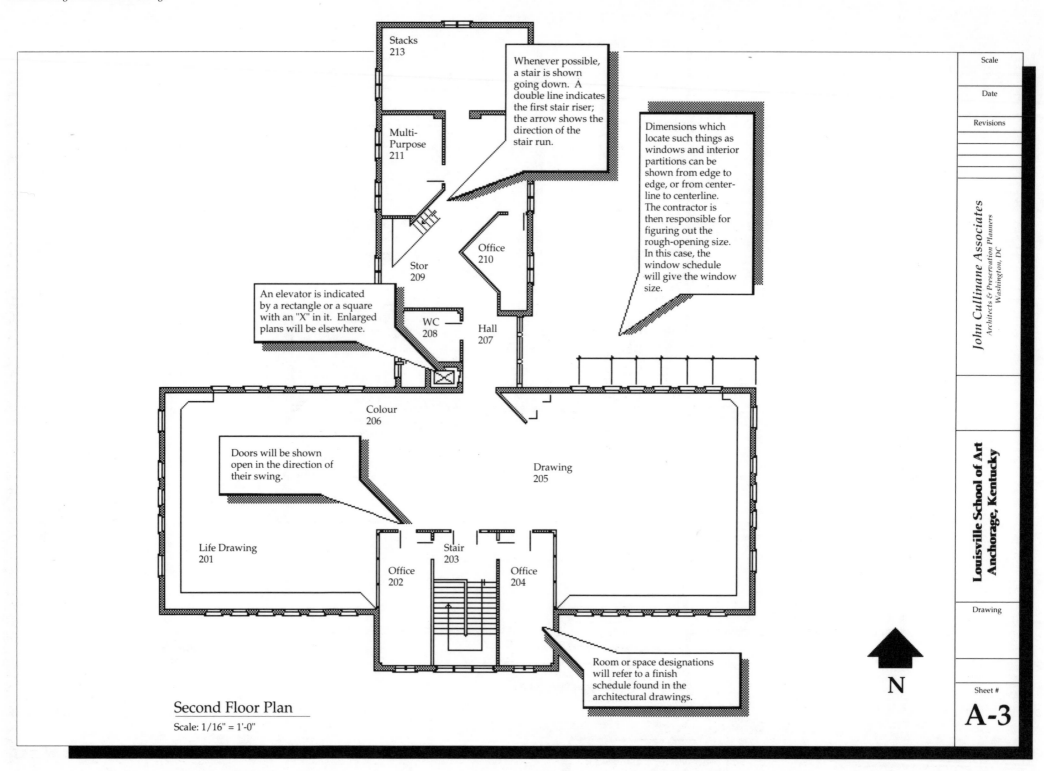

Stacks
213

Whenever possible, a stair is shown going down. A double line indicates the first stair riser; the arrow shows the direction of the stair run.

Multi-Purpose
211

Dimensions which locate such things as windows and interior partitions can be shown from edge to edge, or from center-line to centerline. The contractor is then responsible for figuring out the rough-opening size. In this case, the window schedule will give the window size.

Stor
209

Office
210

An elevator is indicated by a rectangle or a square with an "X" in it. Enlarged plans will be elsewhere.

WC
208

Hall
207

Colour
206

Doors will be shown open in the direction of their swing.

Drawing
205

Life Drawing
201

Stair
203

Office
202

Office
204

Room or space designations will refer to a finish schedule found in the architectural drawings.

N

Second Floor Plan
Scale: 1/16" = 1'-0"

Scale

Date

Revisions

John Cullinane Associates
Architects & Preservation Planners
Washington, DC

Louisville School of Art
Anchorage, Kentucky

Drawing

Sheet #

A-3

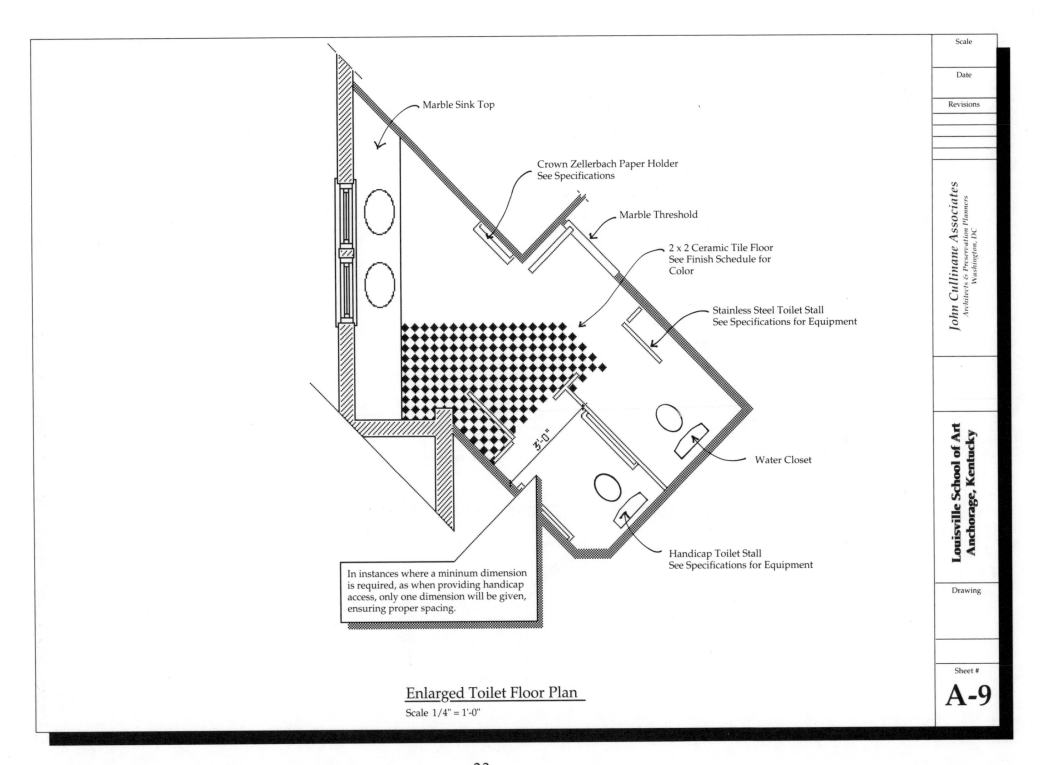

Marble Sink Top

Crown Zellerbach Paper Holder
See Specifications

Marble Threshold

2 x 2 Ceramic Tile Floor
See Finish Schedule for
Color

Stainless Steel Toilet Stall
See Specifications for Equipment

Water Closet

3'-0"

Handicap Toilet Stall
See Specifications for Equipment

In instances where a mininum dimension
is required, as when providing handicap
access, only one dimension will be given,
ensuring proper spacing.

Scale

Date

Revisions

John Cullinane Associates
Architects & Preservation Planners
Washington, DC

Louisville School of Art
Anchorage, Kentucky

Drawing

Sheet #

A-9

Enlarged Toilet Floor Plan
Scale 1/4" = 1'-0"

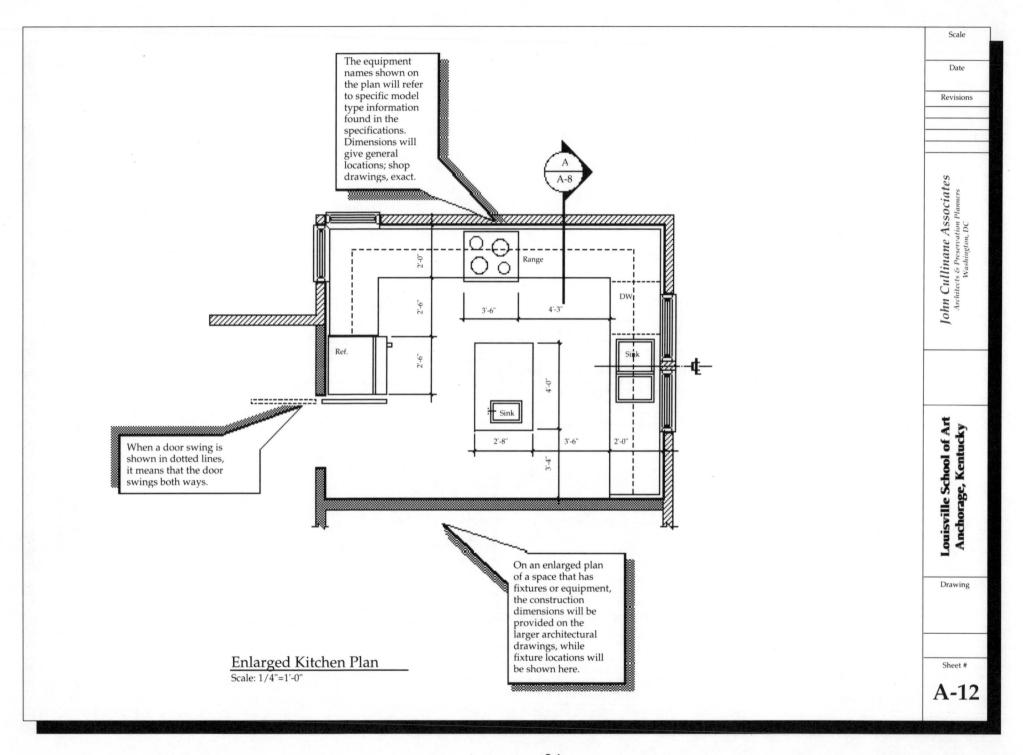

The equipment names shown on the plan will refer to specific model type information found in the specifications. Dimensions will give general locations; shop drawings, exact.

When a door swing is shown in dotted lines, it means that the door swings both ways.

On an enlarged plan of a space that has fixtures or equipment, the construction dimensions will be provided on the larger architectural drawings, while fixture locations will be shown here.

Range

DW

Ref.

Sink

Sink

2'-0"

2'-6"

2'-6"

3'-6"

4'-3"

4'-0"

2'-8"

3'-6"

2'-0"

3'-4"

A
A-8

Enlarged Kitchen Plan
Scale: 1/4"=1'-0"

Scale

Date

Revisions

John Cullinane Associates
*Architects & Preservation Planners
Washington, DC*

**Louisville School of Art
Anchorage, Kentucky**

Drawing

Sheet #

A-12

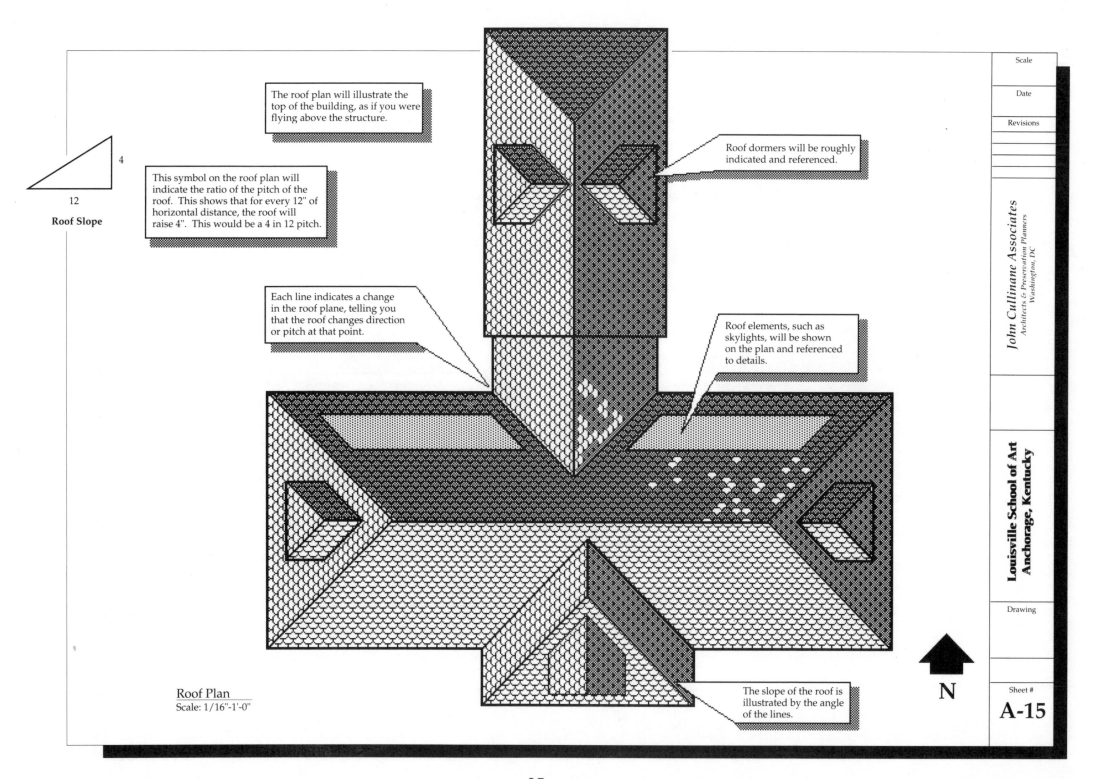

The roof plan will illustrate the top of the building, as if you were flying above the structure.

This symbol on the roof plan will indicate the ratio of the pitch of the roof. This shows that for every 12" of horizontal distance, the roof will raise 4". This would be a 4 in 12 pitch.

Roof Slope

4

12

Roof dormers will be roughly indicated and referenced.

Each line indicates a change in the roof plane, telling you that the roof changes direction or pitch at that point.

Roof elements, such as skylights, will be shown on the plan and referenced to details.

The slope of the roof is illustrated by the angle of the lines.

Roof Plan
Scale: 1/16"-1'-0"

N

Scale

Date

Revisions

John Cullinane Associates
Architects & Preservation Planners
Washington, DC

Louisville School of Art
Anchorage, Kentucky

Drawing

Sheet #
A-15

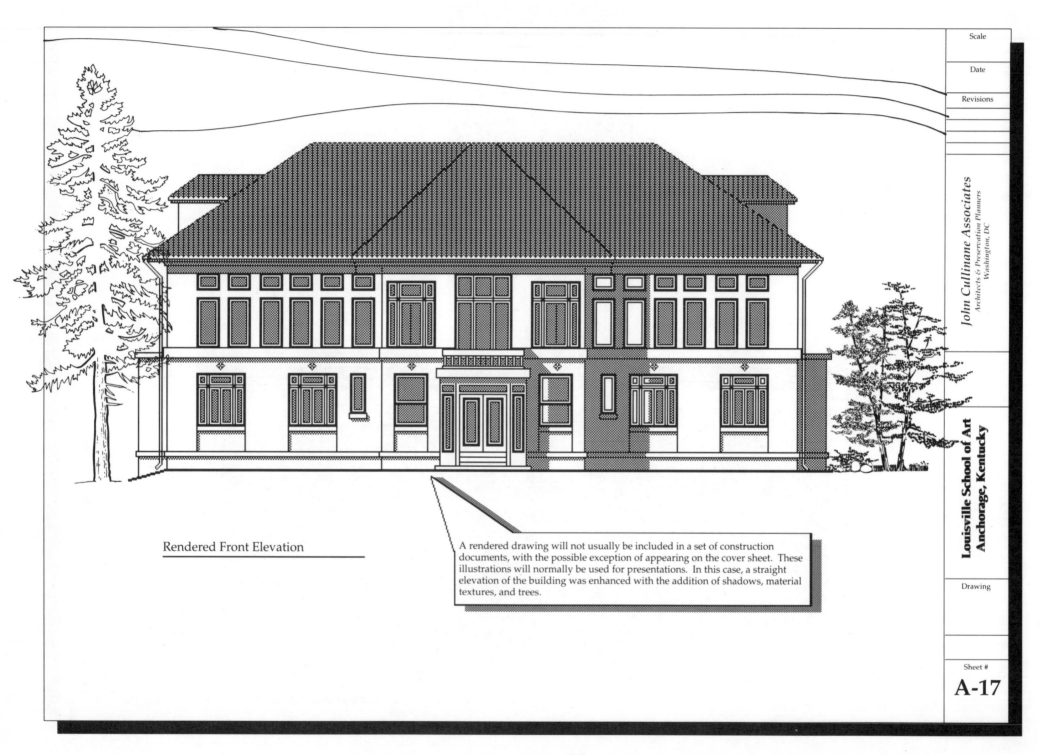

Rendered Front Elevation

A rendered drawing will not usually be included in a set of construction documents, with the possible exception of appearing on the cover sheet. These illustrations will normally be used for presentations. In this case, a straight elevation of the building was enhanced with the addition of shadows, material textures, and trees.

Scale

Date

Revisions

John Cullinane Associates
Architects & Preservation Planners
Washington, DC

Louisville School of Art
Anchorage, Kentucky

Drawing

Sheet #
A-17

Elevation drawings can be extremely deceiving. The problem: they are all drawn in two dimensions, while we generally think in three dimensions. Accordingly, they must be read in conjunction with the floor plans to understand the changes in plane as illustrated on the elevations. A series of elevation drawings will be part of a set of documents. Those elevations following the floor plans usually show all exterior elevations of the building or structure, drawn in the same scale as the plans. Within the set there often will be enlarged plans of portions of the building, such as toilets and kitchens. These will have corresponding elevations of the interior walls and fixtures. Whether illustrating the exterior or interior walls of the building, elevation drawings are developed to provide the contractor with vertical locations of building elements and dimensions, just as the floor plans give horizontal dimensions.

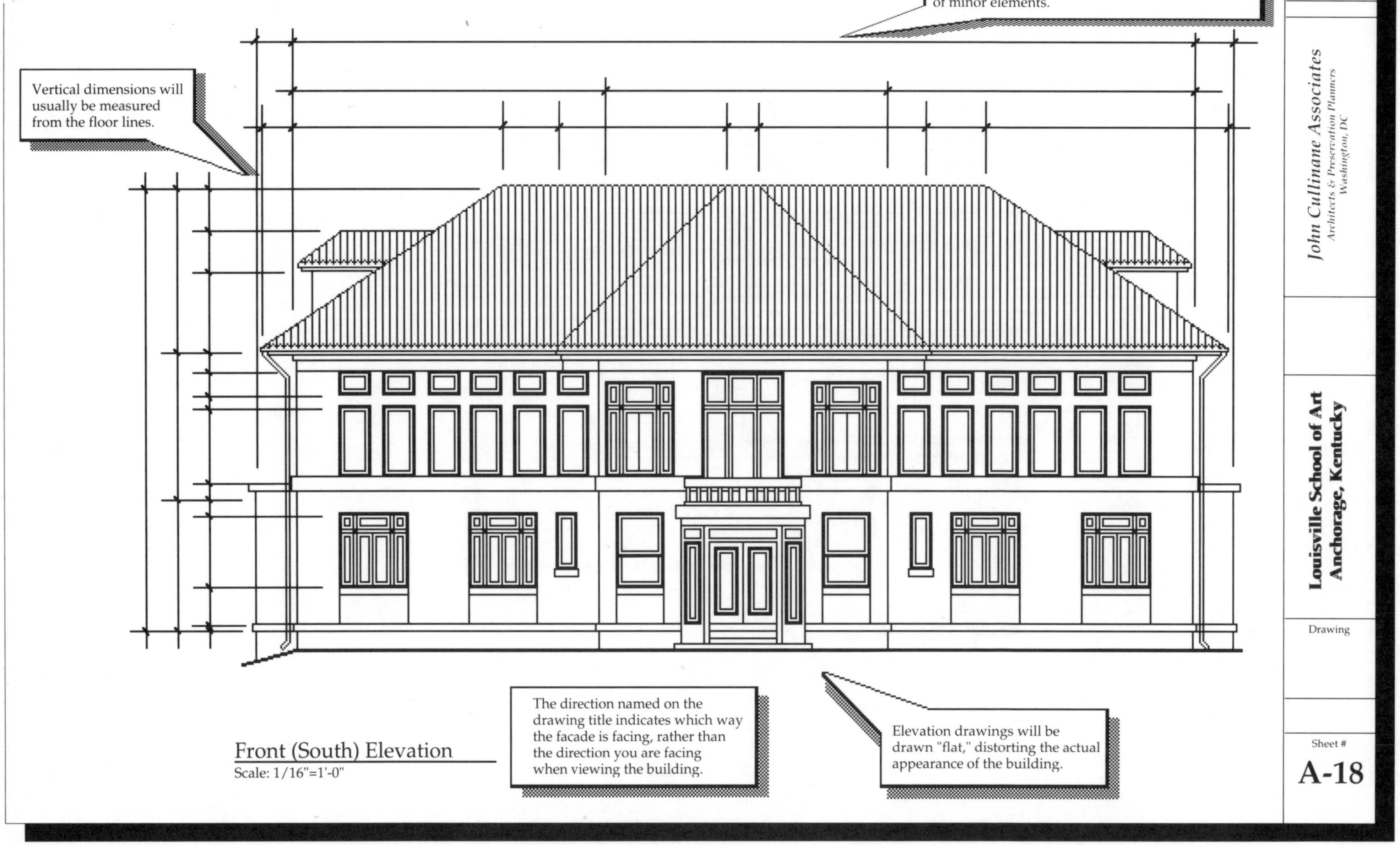

> Dimensions will generally be shown in three levels. The outermost would be the overall size of the structure, the middle string of dimensions would be of major elements, and the inner string would be of minor elements.

> Vertical dimensions will usually be measured from the floor lines.

Front (South) Elevation
Scale: 1/16"=1'-0"

> The direction named on the drawing title indicates which way the facade is facing, rather than the direction you are facing when viewing the building.

> Elevation drawings will be drawn "flat," distorting the actual appearance of the building.

John Cullinane Associates
Architects & Preservation Planners
Washington, DC

Louisville School of Art
Anchorage, Kentucky

Scale

Date

Revisions

Drawing

Sheet #
A-18

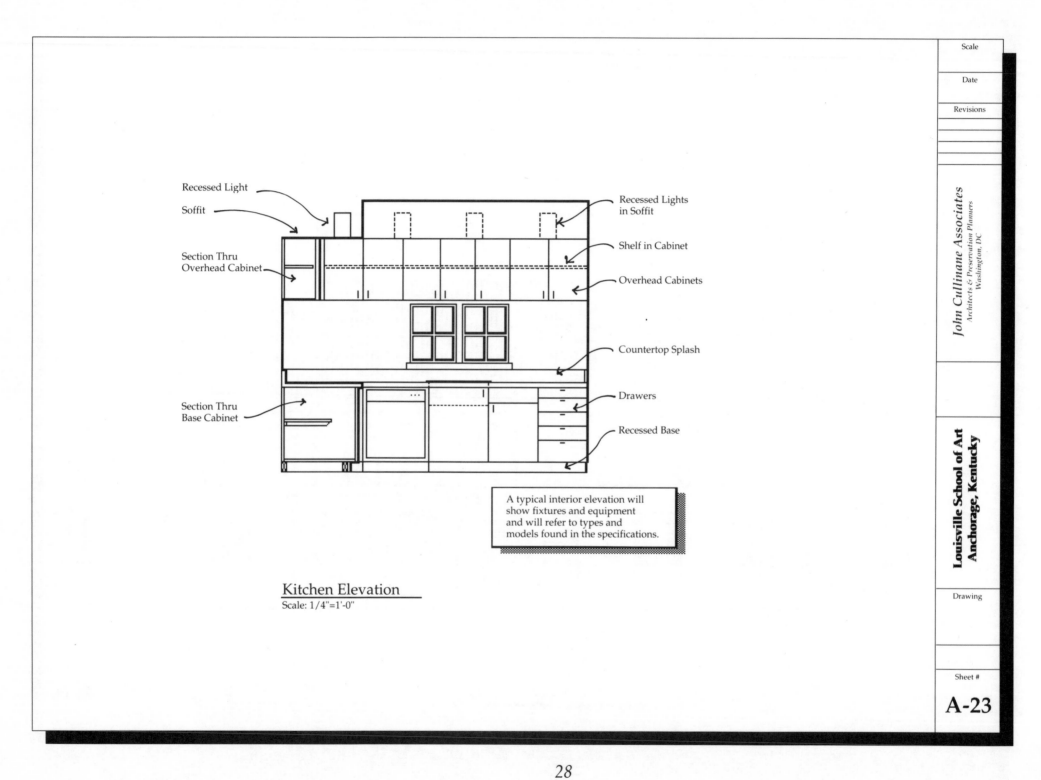

Recessed Light

Soffit

Section Thru
Overhead Cabinet

Section Thru
Base Cabinet

Recessed Lights
in Soffit

Shelf in Cabinet

Overhead Cabinets

Countertop Splash

Drawers

Recessed Base

A typical interior elevation will
show fixtures and equipment
and will refer to types and
models found in the specifications.

Kitchen Elevation
Scale: 1/4"=1'-0"

Scale

Date

Revisions

John Cullinane Associates
Architects & Preservation Planners
Washington, DC

Louisville School of Art
Anchorage, Kentucky

Drawing

Sheet #

A-23

Building sections refer to illustrations showing the entire structure as if it were cut from top to bottom like a piece of cheese. Generally, these sections are drawn at the same scale as the floor plans and elevations and provide a general understanding of the building structure and the vertical relationship of spaces. There may be building sections cut in one or both directions through the building. Most often, building sections will only be included in sets where there are unusual spaces or complex vertical dimensions. They are the type of drawings that the architect will place in the set only if he or she feels that the contractor requires more direction.

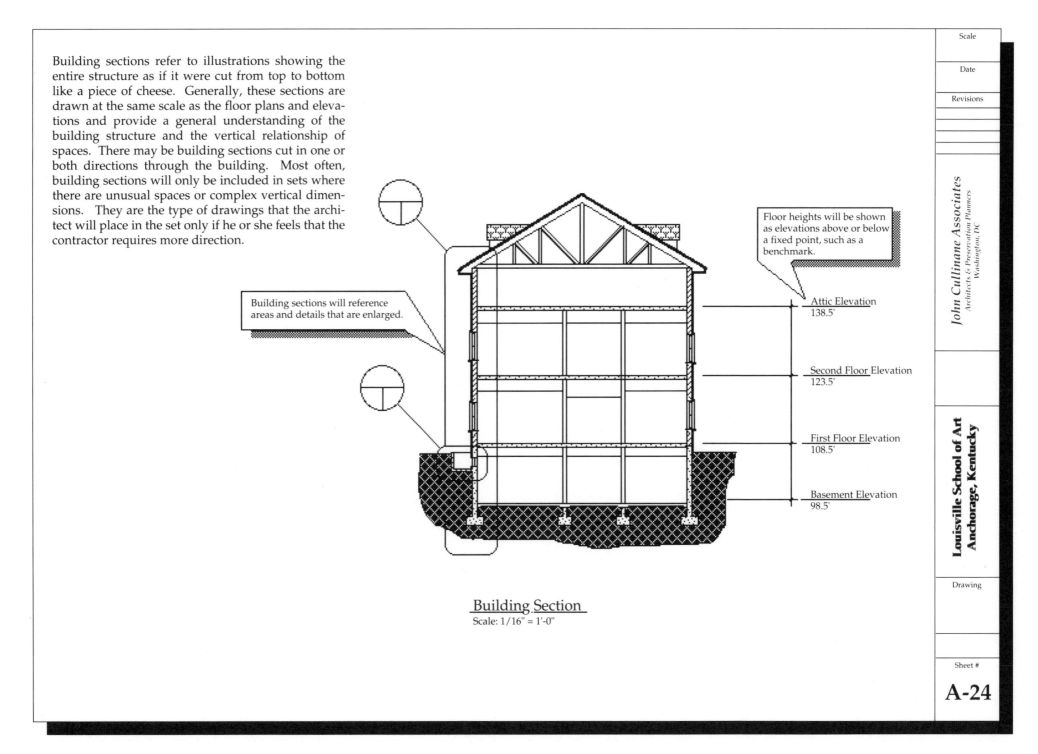

Building sections will reference areas and details that are enlarged.

Floor heights will be shown as elevations above or below a fixed point, such as a benchmark.

Attic Elevation
138.5'

Second Floor Elevation
123.5'

First Floor Elevation
108.5'

Basement Elevation
98.5'

Building Section
Scale: 1/16" = 1'-0"

Scale

Date

Revisions

John Cullinane Associates
Architects & Preservation Planners
Washington, DC

Louisville School of Art
Anchorage, Kentucky

Drawing

Sheet #

A-24

Wall sections will be drawn in a number of different scales but always larger than the floor plans. These are designed to provide the contractor with detailed information on the relationship of building elements in the exterior, and sometimes interior, walls. The sections can illustrate the entire wall, from foundation to roof, or they can isolate a single portion of the wall. At times the wall section will be used as an index for larger-scale details, such as drawings of intersections between floors and walls or roof joints. When viewing a set of drawings, remember, the larger the scale and the more detailed a drawing, the more authority. In the determination of how to construct a building, a large-scale detail of a floor connection takes precedence over the same connection shown in a wall section, which takes precedence over that same connection shown in a building section.

Face Brick

Wallboard

Recessed Base

Finished Floor

Subfloor

Flashing

Earth

Waterproofing

Wood Blocking

Wood Floor Joists

Reinforced Foundation Wall

Concrete Slab on Grade

Reinforcing Bars

Foundation Drain

Spread Footing

Partial Wall Section
Scale: 3/4"=1'-0"

Scale

Date

Revisions

John Cullinane Associates
Architects & Preservation Planners
Washington, DC

Louisville School of Art
Anchorage, Kentucky

Drawing

Sheet #

A-30

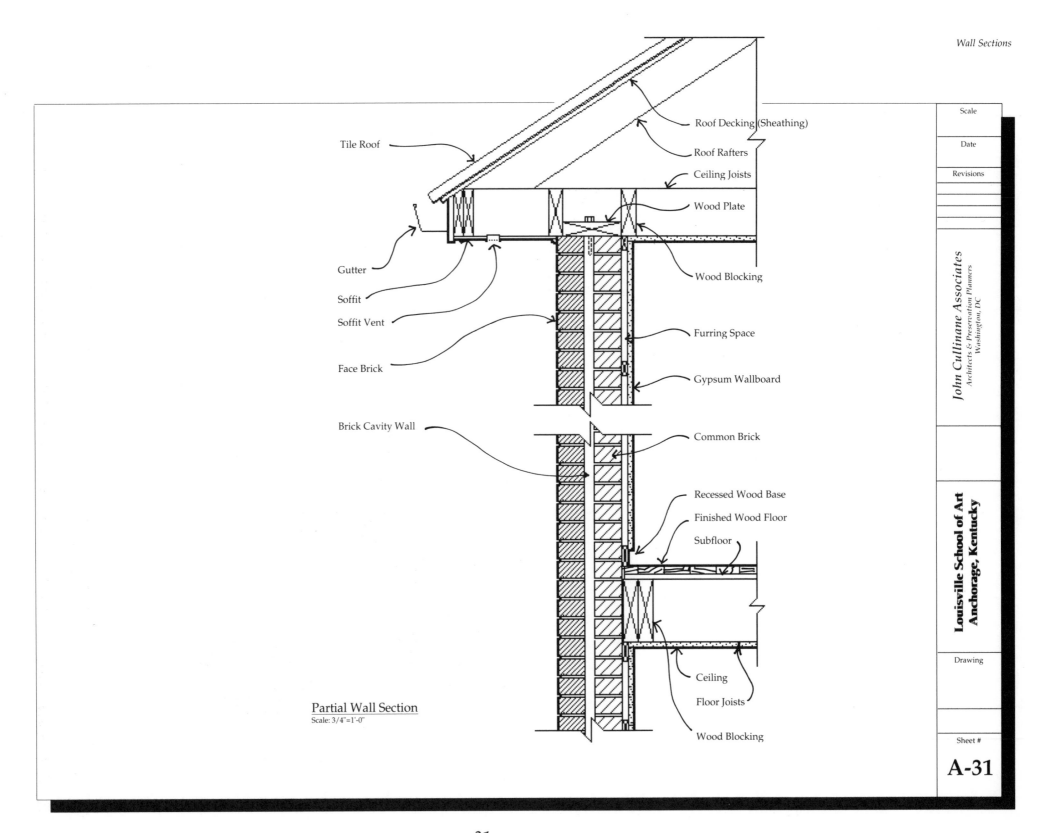

Roof Decking (Sheathing)

Tile Roof

Roof Rafters

Ceiling Joists

Wood Plate

Gutter

Wood Blocking

Soffit

Soffit Vent

Furring Space

Face Brick

Gypsum Wallboard

Brick Cavity Wall

Common Brick

Recessed Wood Base

Finished Wood Floor

Subfloor

Ceiling

Floor Joists

Wood Blocking

Partial Wall Section
Scale: 3/4"=1'-0"

Scale

Date

Revisions

John Cullinane Associates
Architects & Preservation Planners
Washington, DC

Louisville School of Art
Anchorage, Kentucky

Drawing

Sheet #

A-31

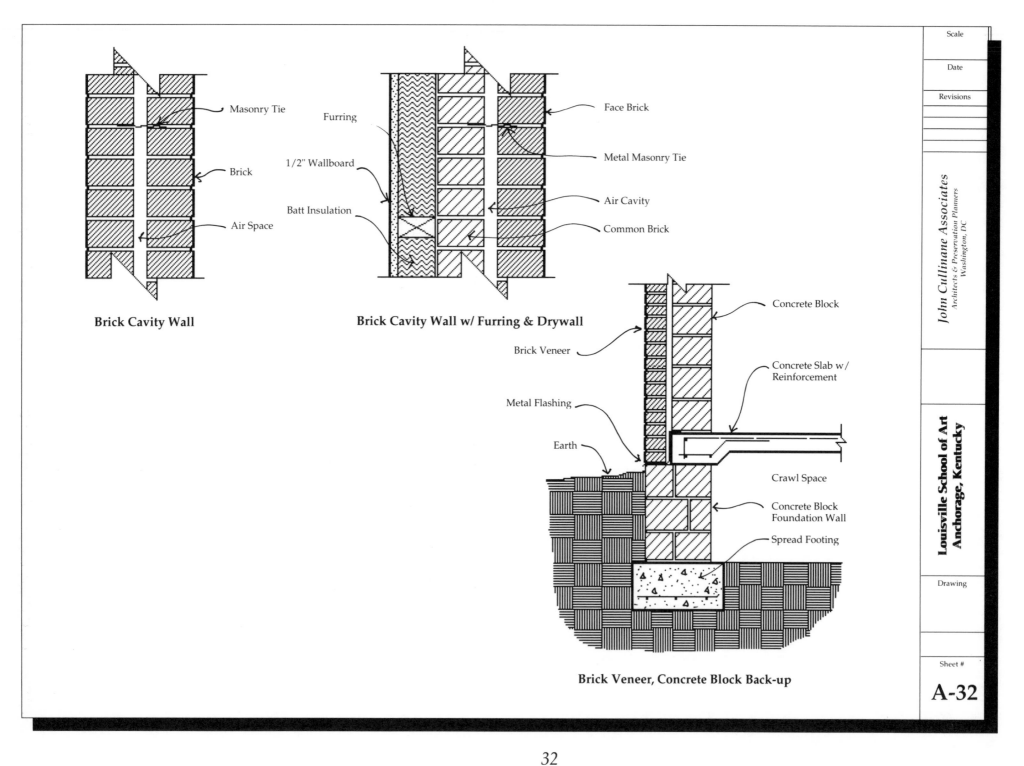

Brick Cavity Wall

Masonry Tie

Brick

Air Space

Brick Cavity Wall w/ Furring & Drywall

Furring

1/2" Wallboard

Batt Insulation

Face Brick

Metal Masonry Tie

Air Cavity

Common Brick

Brick Veneer, Concrete Block Back-up

Concrete Block

Brick Veneer

Concrete Slab w/ Reinforcement

Metal Flashing

Earth

Crawl Space

Concrete Block Foundation Wall

Spread Footing

Scale

Date

Revisions

John Cullinane Associates
Architects & Preservation Planners
Washington, DC

Louisville School of Art
Anchorage, Kentucky

Drawing

Sheet #

A-32

At times the configuration or construction of the ceiling in a particular space within a building will be so complex or important that the architect feels detailed illustrations are necessary to guide the contractor. In some cases the location of light fixtures, fire-protection elements, such as sprinkler heads, and air diffusers may be critical to the design of the space. In these instances, plans of the ceilings will be included in the drawing set and referred to as "reflected ceiling plans." They are drawn as if the architect were imitating Michelangelo, lying on his or her back about a foot from the ceiling and looking up. The primary purpose of these drawings is to eliminate questions and options for locating elements in the ceiling and to direct the contractor or subcontractor accordingly.

Ceiling Diffuser

An "equal" note will indicate that the spaces on either side of the room are to be the same dimension.

Recessed Light Fixtures

Acoustic Tile

A reflected ceiling plan is an illustration of the ceiling of a room or space shown as if you were lying on your back looking up to the ceiling.

Toilet Reflected Ceiling Plan
Scale: 1/4"=1'-0"

Scale
Date
Revisions

John Cullinane Associates
Architects & Preservation Planners
Washington, DC

Louisville School of Art
Anchorage, Kentucky

Drawing

Sheet #

A-35

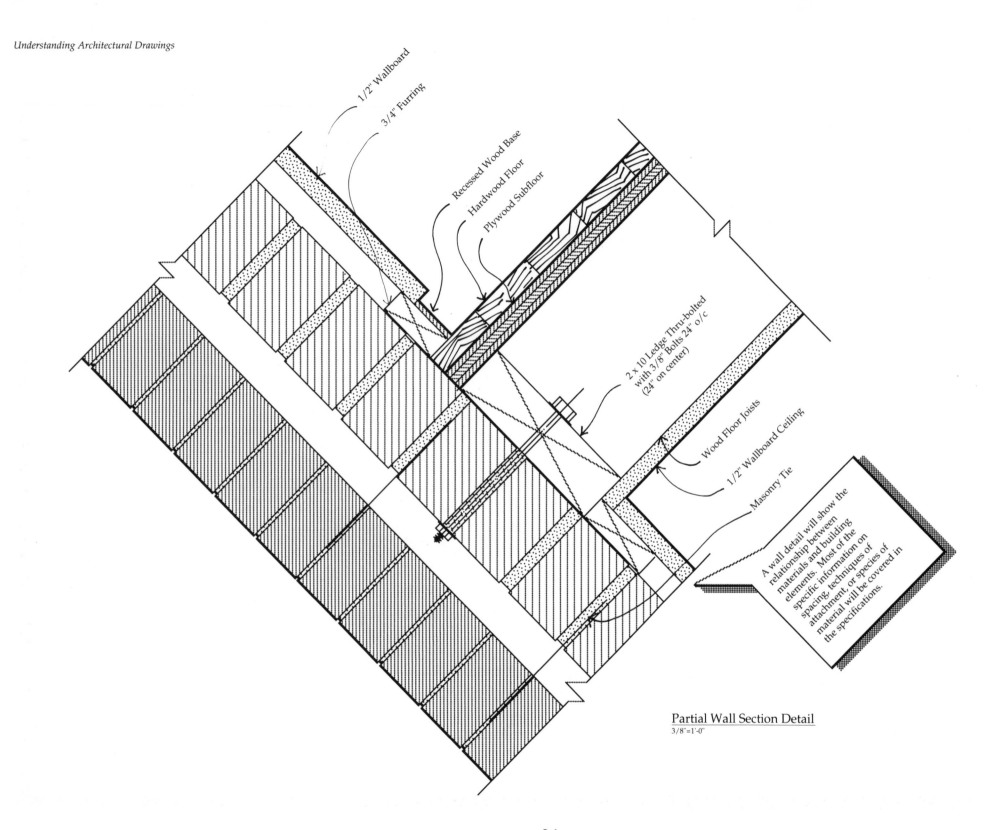

1/2" Wallboard

3/4" Furring

Recessed Wood Base

Hardwood Floor

Plywood Subfloor

2 x 10 Ledge Thru-bolted with 3/8" Bolts 24" o/c (24" on center)

Wood Floor Joists

1/2" Wallboard Ceiling

Masonry Tie

A wall detail will show the relationship between materials and building elements. Most of the specific information on spacing, techniques of attachment, or species of material will be covered in the specifications.

Partial Wall Section Detail
3/8"=1'-0"

As the composition of a set of drawings proceeds from general, gross scale to specific, detailed scale, so does the design process. After the initial concept design of a new building or rehabilitation project is complete, design development is initiated. This is the process by which all of the details of how to execute the work is developed. The enlarged details in a set of drawings represent the product of the design-development process. The theory is that the larger the scale of the drawing, the more accurate the illustration. Accordingly, a great amount of thought is used in drawing the details of a project. Detail drawings of general construction will appear in the set after the plans and elevations. Drawings related to specific systems, such as doors and windows, will be shown with schedules. The scale of detail drawings will range from 1/2″ and 3/4″= 1′-0″ to 1-1/2″ and 3″ = 1′-0″ (at times the later two will be noted as 1/8 Full Scale or 1/4 FS, respectively).

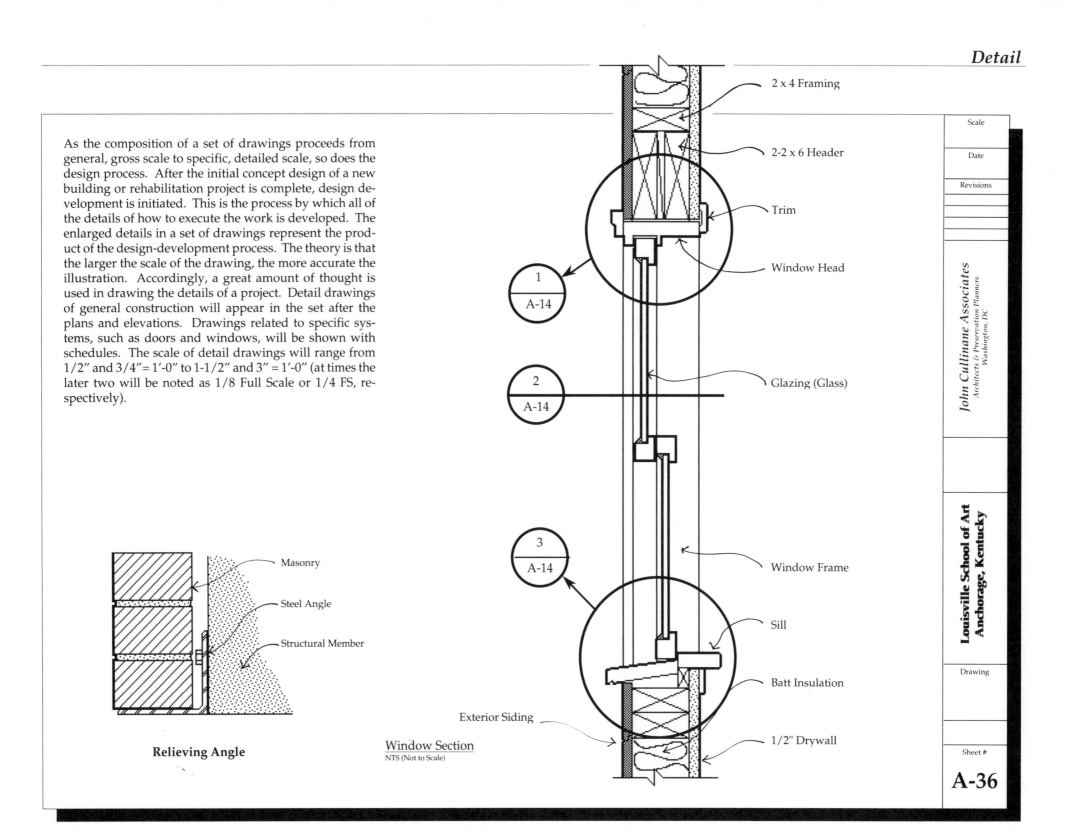

Relieving Angle

Window Section
NTS (Not to Scale)

2 x 4 Framing

2-2 x 6 Header

Trim

Window Head

1 / A-14

2 / A-14

Glazing (Glass)

3 / A-14

Window Frame

Sill

Batt Insulation

Exterior Siding

1/2″ Drywall

Masonry

Steel Angle

Structural Member

John Cullinane Associates
Architects & Preservation Planners
Washington, DC

Louisville School of Art
Anchorage, Kentucky

Scale

Date

Revisions

Drawing

Sheet #

A-36

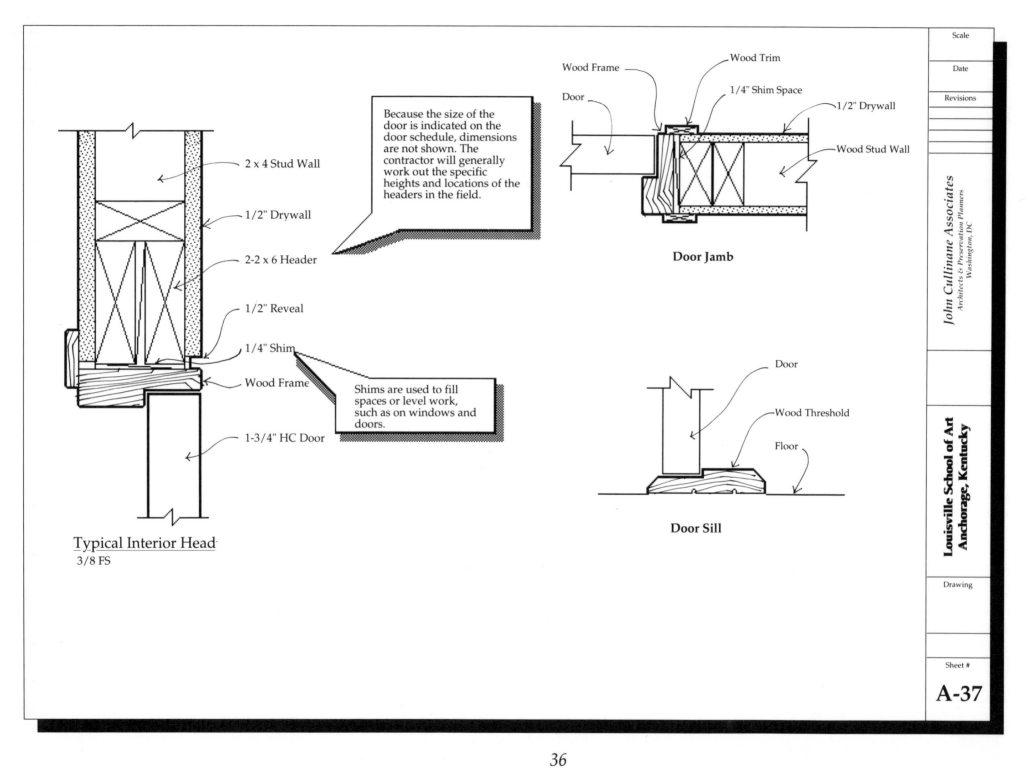

2 x 4 Stud Wall

1/2" Drywall

2-2 x 6 Header

1/2" Reveal

1/4" Shim

Wood Frame

1-3/4" HC Door

Because the size of the door is indicated on the door schedule, dimensions are not shown. The contractor will generally work out the specific heights and locations of the headers in the field.

Shims are used to fill spaces or level work, such as on windows and doors.

Typical Interior Head
3/8 FS

Wood Frame

Wood Trim

1/4" Shim Space

Door

1/2" Drywall

Wood Stud Wall

Door Jamb

Door

Wood Threshold

Floor

Door Sill

Scale

Date

Revisions

John Cullinane Associates
Architects & Preservation Planners
Washington, DC

Louisville School of Art
Anchorage, Kentucky

Drawing

Sheet #

A-37

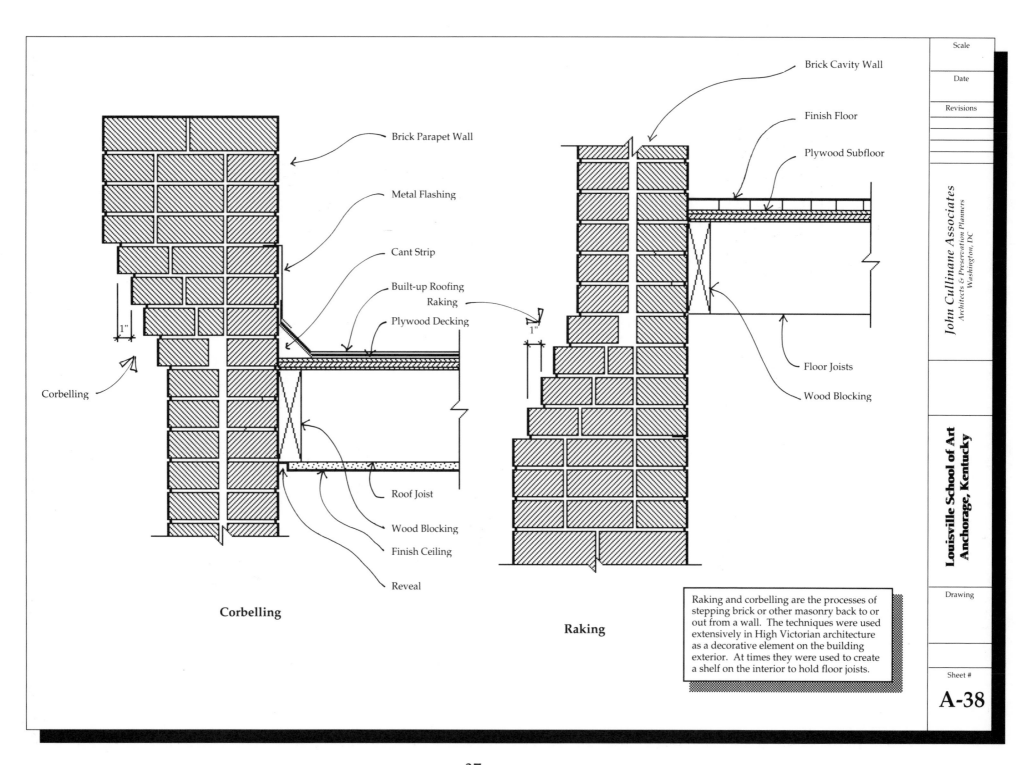

Corbelling

Brick Parapet Wall

Metal Flashing

Cant Strip

Built-up Roofing

Raking

Plywood Decking

Corbelling

1"

Roof Joist

Wood Blocking

Finish Ceiling

Reveal

Raking

Brick Cavity Wall

Finish Floor

Plywood Subfloor

Floor Joists

Wood Blocking

1"

Raking and corbelling are the processes of stepping brick or other masonry back to or out from a wall. The techniques were used extensively in High Victorian architecture as a decorative element on the building exterior. At times they were used to create a shelf on the interior to hold floor joists.

John Cullinane Associates
Architects & Preservation Planners
Washington, DC

Louisville School of Art
Anchorage, Kentucky

Scale

Date

Revisions

Drawing

Sheet #

A-38

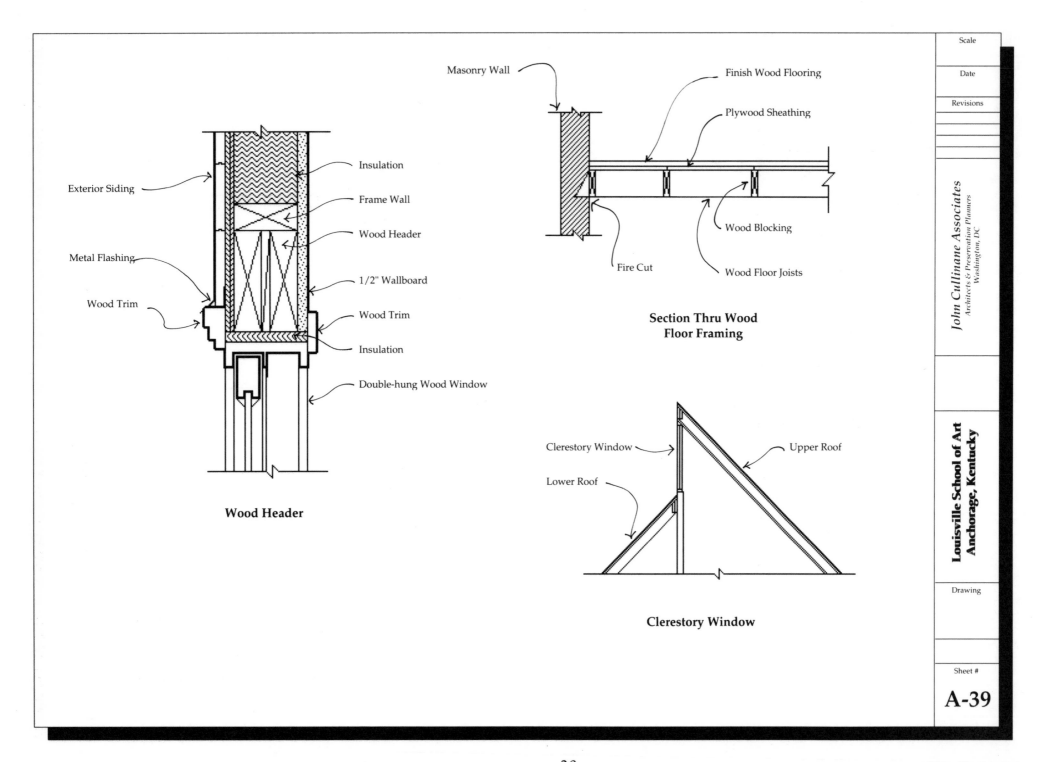

Exterior Siding

Insulation

Frame Wall

Metal Flashing

Wood Header

Wood Trim

1/2" Wallboard

Wood Trim

Insulation

Double-hung Wood Window

Wood Header

Masonry Wall

Finish Wood Flooring

Plywood Sheathing

Wood Blocking

Fire Cut

Wood Floor Joists

**Section Thru Wood
Floor Framing**

Clerestory Window

Upper Roof

Lower Roof

Clerestory Window

Scale

Date

Revisions

John Cullinane Associates
Architects & Preservation Planners
Washington, DC

**Louisville School of Art
Anchorage, Kentucky**

Drawing

Sheet #

A-39

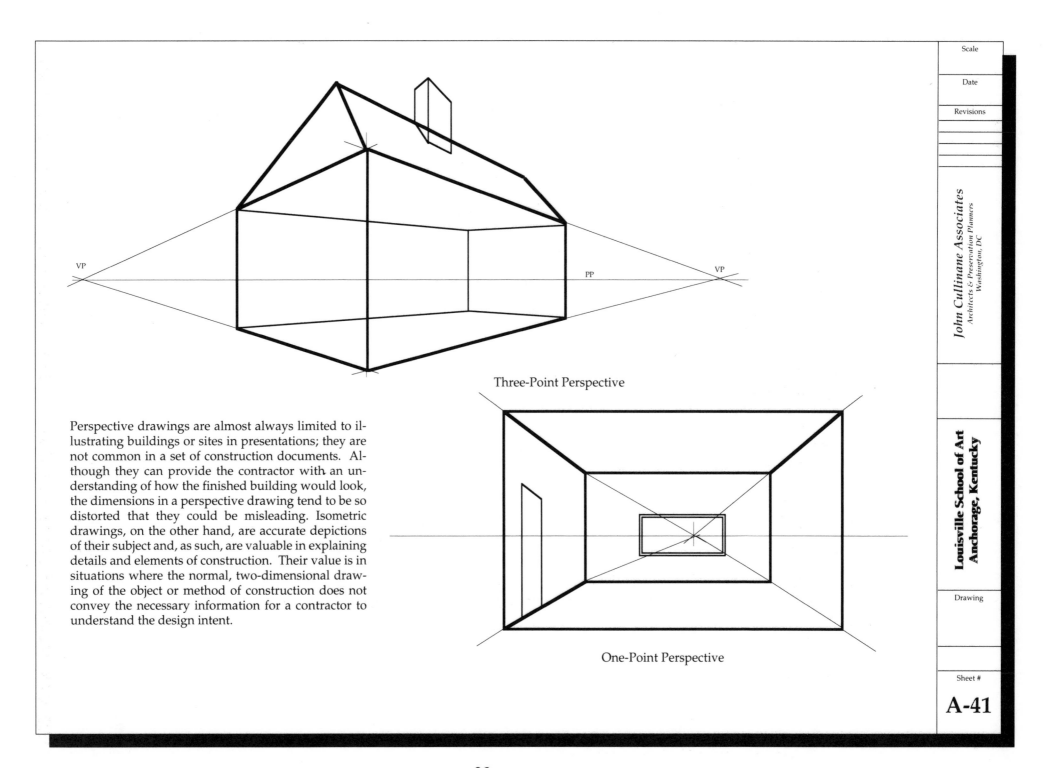

Three-Point Perspective

Perspective drawings are almost always limited to illustrating buildings or sites in presentations; they are not common in a set of construction documents. Although they can provide the contractor with an understanding of how the finished building would look, the dimensions in a perspective drawing tend to be so distorted that they could be misleading. Isometric drawings, on the other hand, are accurate depictions of their subject and, as such, are valuable in explaining details and elements of construction. Their value is in situations where the normal, two-dimensional drawing of the object or method of construction does not convey the necessary information for a contractor to understand the design intent.

One-Point Perspective

VP   PP   VP

Scale

Date

Revisions

John Cullinane Associates
Architects & Preservation Planners
Washington, DC

Louisville School of Art
Anchorage, Kentucky

Drawing

Sheet #

A-41

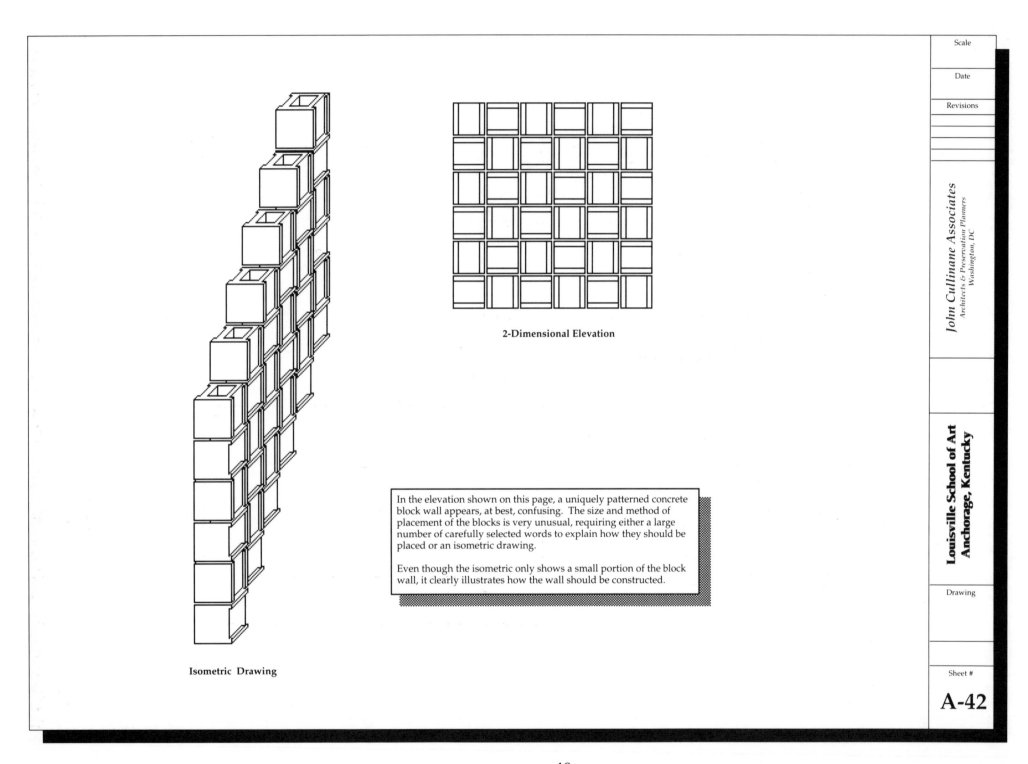

2-Dimensional Elevation

Isometric Drawing

In the elevation shown on this page, a uniquely patterned concrete block wall appears, at best, confusing. The size and method of placement of the blocks is very unusual, requiring either a large number of carefully selected words to explain how they should be placed or an isometric drawing.

Even though the isometric only shows a small portion of the block wall, it clearly illustrates how the wall should be constructed.

Scale

Date

Revisions

John Cullinane Associates
Architects & Preservation Planners
Washington, DC

Louisville School of Art
Anchorage, Kentucky

Drawing

Sheet #

A-42

With the exception of some small residential projects, architects will have structural engineers design and draw the structural system for a building. Structural drawings will appear immediately after the basic architectural floor plans, and, as with electrical and mechanical drawings, will generally be superimposed on halftones of the architectural plans. The quantity of structural drawings depends on the complexity of the building and its support system. For a simple post and beam structural system in a building there would be just basic plans, beam schedules, and details. For a unique structure that may require exotic systems, such as space frames, there would be extensive drawings and detailing, all developed to ensure that the contractor correctly sizes and installs structural elements. Unlike electrical and plumbing systems, structural drawings leave very little, if anything, for the contractor to work out in the field. The sizing and placement of structural members is critical to supporting the structure and in ensuring the safety of its users.

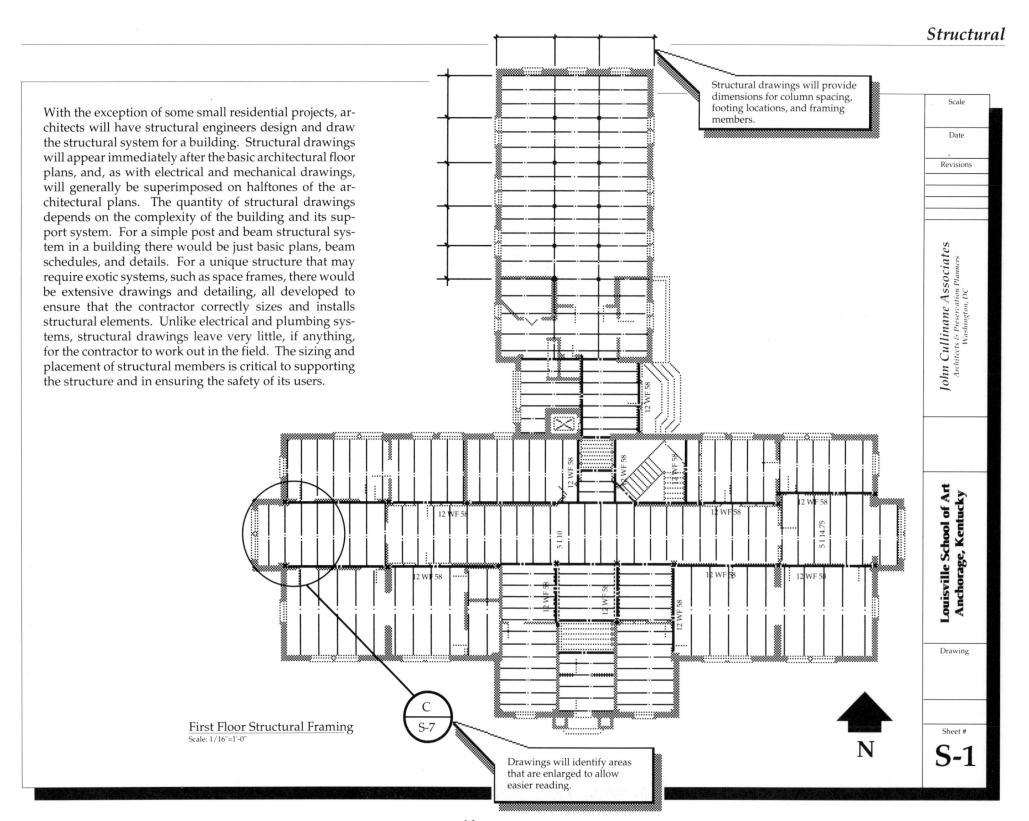

Structural drawings will provide dimensions for column spacing, footing locations, and framing members.

First Floor Structural Framing
Scale: 1/16"=1'-0"

C
S-7

Drawings will identify areas that are enlarged to allow easier reading.

N

Scale

Date

Revisions

John Cullinane Associates
Architects & Preservation Planners
Washington, DC

Louisville School of Art
Anchorage, Kentucky

Drawing

Sheet #

S-1

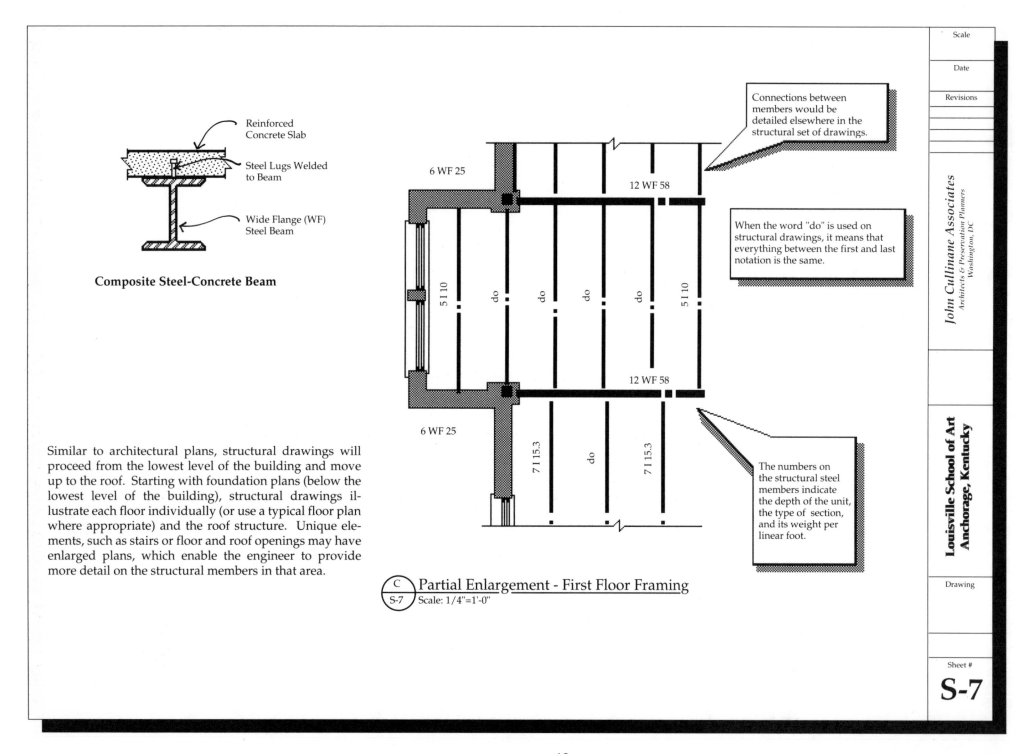

Reinforced Concrete Slab

Steel Lugs Welded to Beam

Wide Flange (WF) Steel Beam

Composite Steel-Concrete Beam

Connections between members would be detailed elsewhere in the structural set of drawings.

6 WF 25

12 WF 58

When the word "do" is used on structural drawings, it means that everything between the first and last notation is the same.

5 I 10

do

do

do

do

5 I 10

12 WF 58

6 WF 25

7 I 15.3

do

7 I 15.3

The numbers on the structural steel members indicate the depth of the unit, the type of section, and its weight per linear foot.

Similar to architectural plans, structural drawings will proceed from the lowest level of the building and move up to the roof. Starting with foundation plans (below the lowest level of the building), structural drawings illustrate each floor individually (or use a typical floor plan where appropriate) and the roof structure. Unique elements, such as stairs or floor and roof openings may have enlarged plans, which enable the engineer to provide more detail on the structural members in that area.

C
S-7
Partial Enlargement - First Floor Framing
Scale: 1/4"=1'-0"

John Cullinane Associates
Architects & Preservation Planners
Washington, DC

**Louisville School of Art
Anchorage, Kentucky**

Scale

Date

Revisions

Drawing

Sheet #

S-7

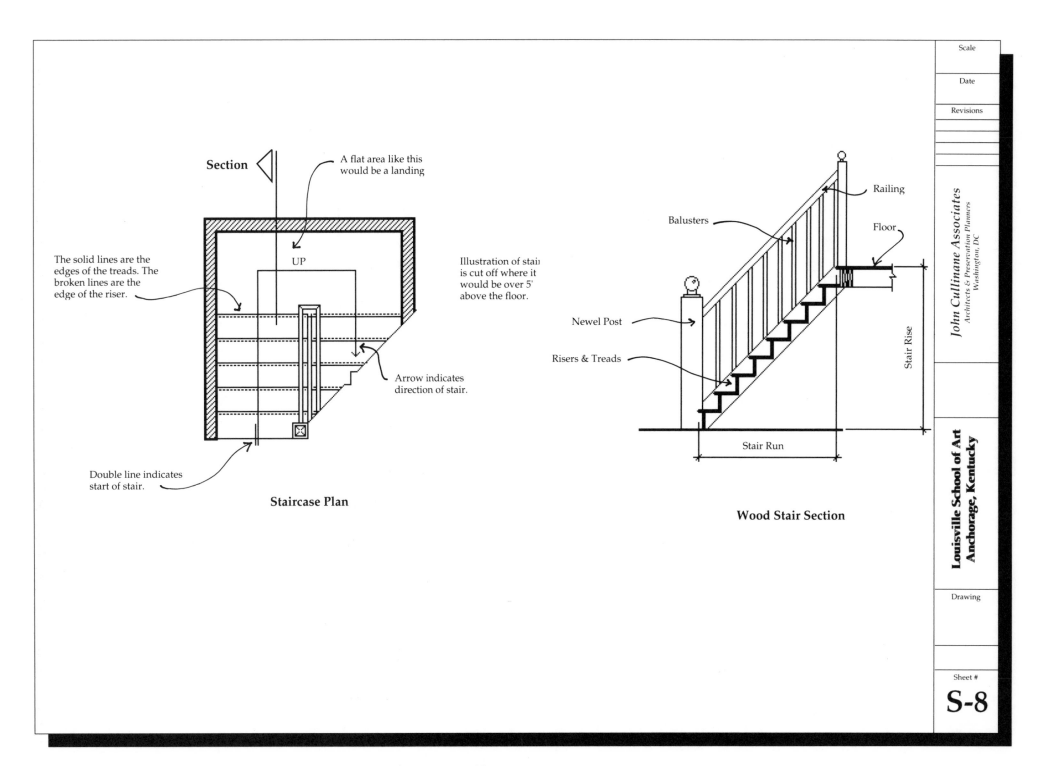

Section

A flat area like this would be a landing

UP

The solid lines are the edges of the treads. The broken lines are the edge of the riser.

Illustration of stair is cut off where it would be over 5' above the floor.

Arrow indicates direction of stair.

Double line indicates start of stair.

Staircase Plan

Railing

Balusters

Floor

Newel Post

Stair Rise

Risers & Treads

Stair Run

Wood Stair Section

John Cullinane Associates
Architects & Preservation Planners
Washington, DC

Louisville School of Art
Anchorage, Kentucky

Scale

Date

Revisions

Drawing

Sheet #

S-8

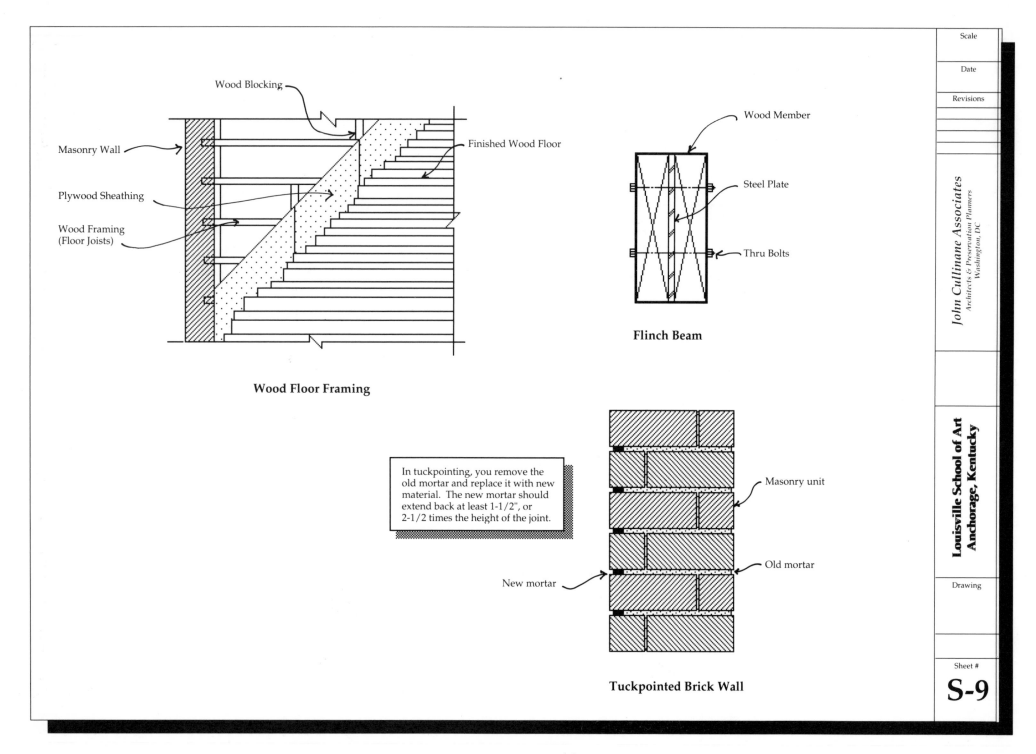

Wood Blocking

Masonry Wall

Plywood Sheathing

Wood Framing
(Floor Joists)

Finished Wood Floor

Wood Floor Framing

Wood Member

Steel Plate

Thru Bolts

Flinch Beam

In tuckpointing, you remove the
old mortar and replace it with new
material. The new mortar should
extend back at least 1-1/2", or
2-1/2 times the height of the joint.

Masonry unit

Old mortar

New mortar

Tuckpointed Brick Wall

Scale

Date

Revisions

John Cullinane Associates
Architects & Preservation Planners
Washington, DC

Louisville School of Art
Anchorage, Kentucky

Drawing

Sheet #

S-9

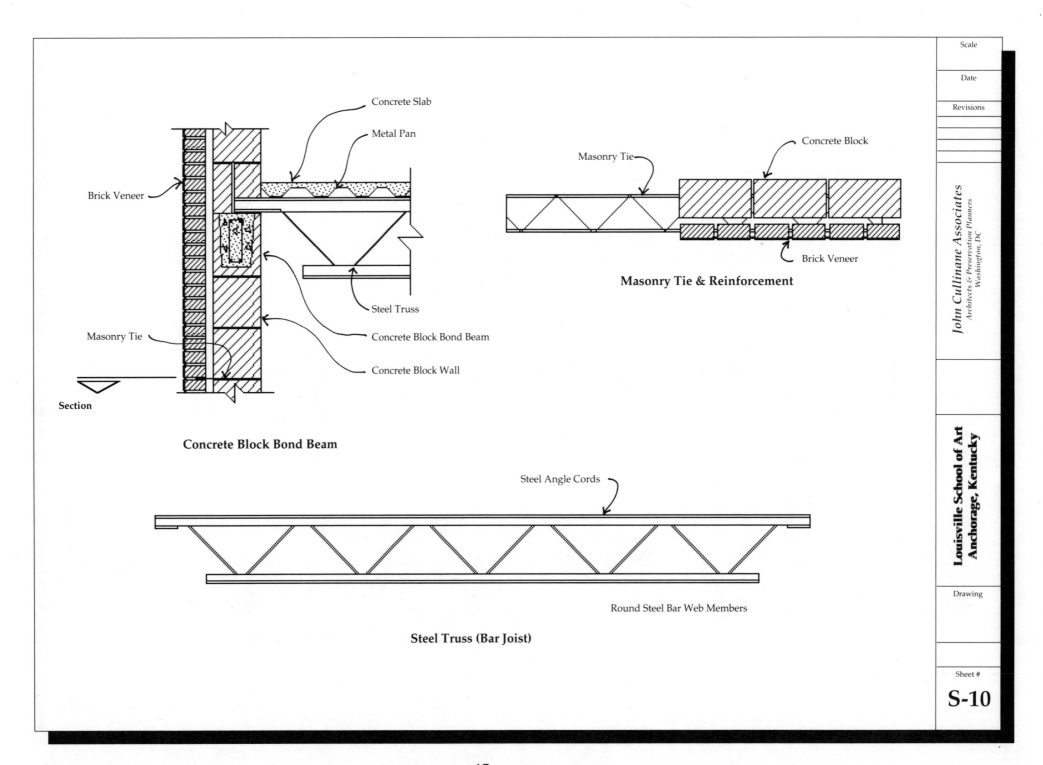

Concrete Slab

Metal Pan

Brick Veneer

Masonry Tie

Steel Truss

Concrete Block Bond Beam

Concrete Block Wall

Section

Concrete Block Bond Beam

Concrete Block

Masonry Tie

Brick Veneer

Masonry Tie & Reinforcement

Steel Angle Cords

Round Steel Bar Web Members

Steel Truss (Bar Joist)

Scale

Date

Revisions

John Cullinane Associates
Architects & Preservation Planners
Washington, DC

Louisville School of Art
Anchorage, Kentucky

Drawing

Sheet #

S-10

45

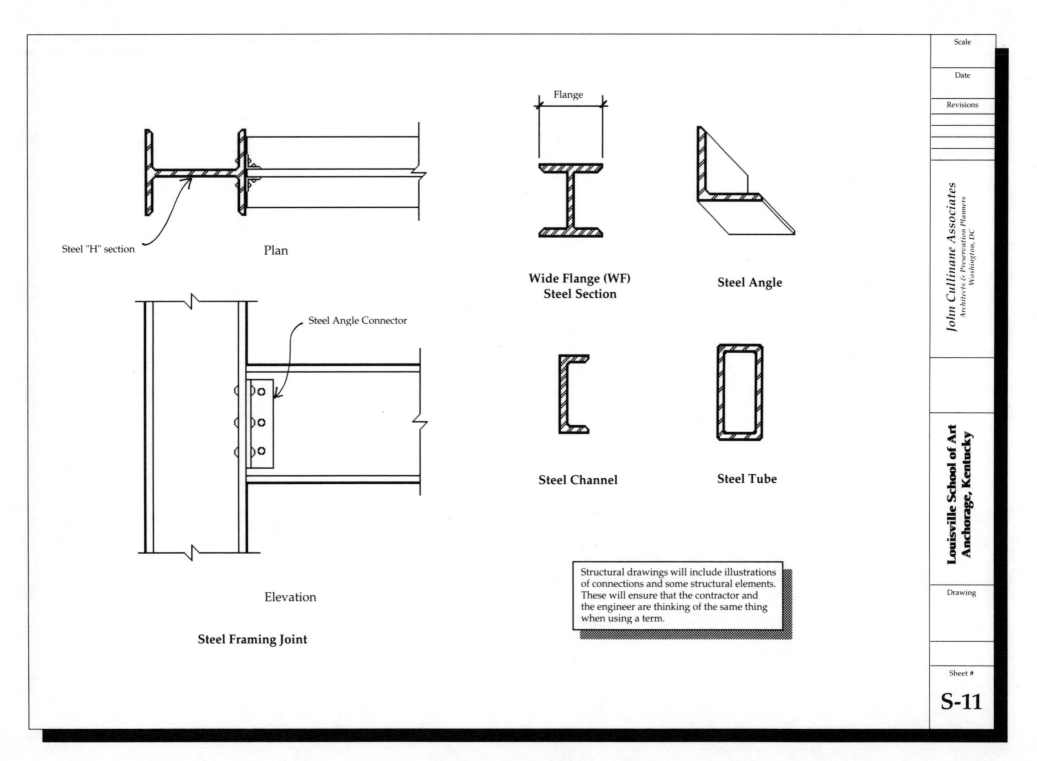

Steel "H" section

Plan

Steel Angle Connector

Elevation

Steel Framing Joint

Flange

**Wide Flange (WF)
Steel Section**

Steel Angle

Steel Channel

Steel Tube

Structural drawings will include illustrations
of connections and some structural elements.
These will ensure that the contractor and
the engineer are thinking of the same thing
when using a term.

Scale
Date
Revisions

John Cullinane Associates
Architects & Preservation Planners
Washington, DC

**Louisville School of Art
Anchorage, Kentucky**

Drawing

Sheet #

S-11

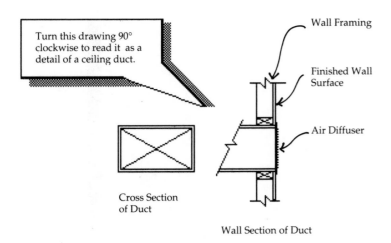

Turn this drawing 90° clockwise to read it as a detail of a ceiling duct.

Cross Section of Duct

Wall Section of Duct

Wall Framing

Finished Wall Surface

Air Diffuser

Duct & Ductwork

Mechanical systems and drawings are an enigma to most architects. They know that the mechanical system is essential to the operation and function of their building, but they would be hard pressed to explain exactly how it works or why it was designed the way it was. Aside from the structural frame and architectural details, the mechanical system will represent the greatest design effort and monetary investment in a building. Depending on the use of the building, mechanical systems can account for from 30 percent to 60 percent of the total building cost.

The mechanical engineer, usually depicted as a creature with many arms and eyes in architecture cartoons, is responsible for ensuring that occupants of a simple structure are supplied with all necessary conditioned air and water to allow them to function as required by the building program. In a complex building, such as a research laboratory or a hospital, the engineer has the additional burden of designing negative- or positive-pressure spaces, piping gases in and out of the structure, and ensuring that contaminated waste, whether air or liquid, is removed without endangering occupants or users.

Unlike electrical drawings and specifications, which rely heavily on standard techniques, code requirements, and standards to ensure proper installation, mechanical systems will be customized for each building. There are, of course, standard methods of connecting ducts and hanging pipes, but the size of the ducts and pipes, their configuration, and all of the air and water pumping systems are unique to that installation. Thus, no two sets of mechanical drawings will look the same.

The mechanical engineer generally uses halftones of the architectural drawings as a base on which to superimpose the duct and piping layout. Detailed drawings of machinery and connections are included in the set.

General mechanical plans illustrate air supply and piping both below and above the floor plan on which they are shown. The type of line drawn indicates the location of the equipment.

Piping and fixtures for plumbing in the building will often be a subset of the mechanical drawings. The plumbing system will usually be designed by the same engineer and, because the water supply and waste piping are so interlocked with the same requirements for mechanical systems, it is logical that they share the same set of drawings. Although the piping for a building will be unique to its design and use, plumbing fixtures have been standardized for many years. The form and size of kitchen, toilet, bathroom, and utility fixtures are all drawn using templates. These tools have traditionally been provided to architects and engineers free of charge by none other than plumbing fixture manufacturers.

Plumbing drawings, using halftones of the architectural plans, generally show piping and fixtures on or below the floor shown.

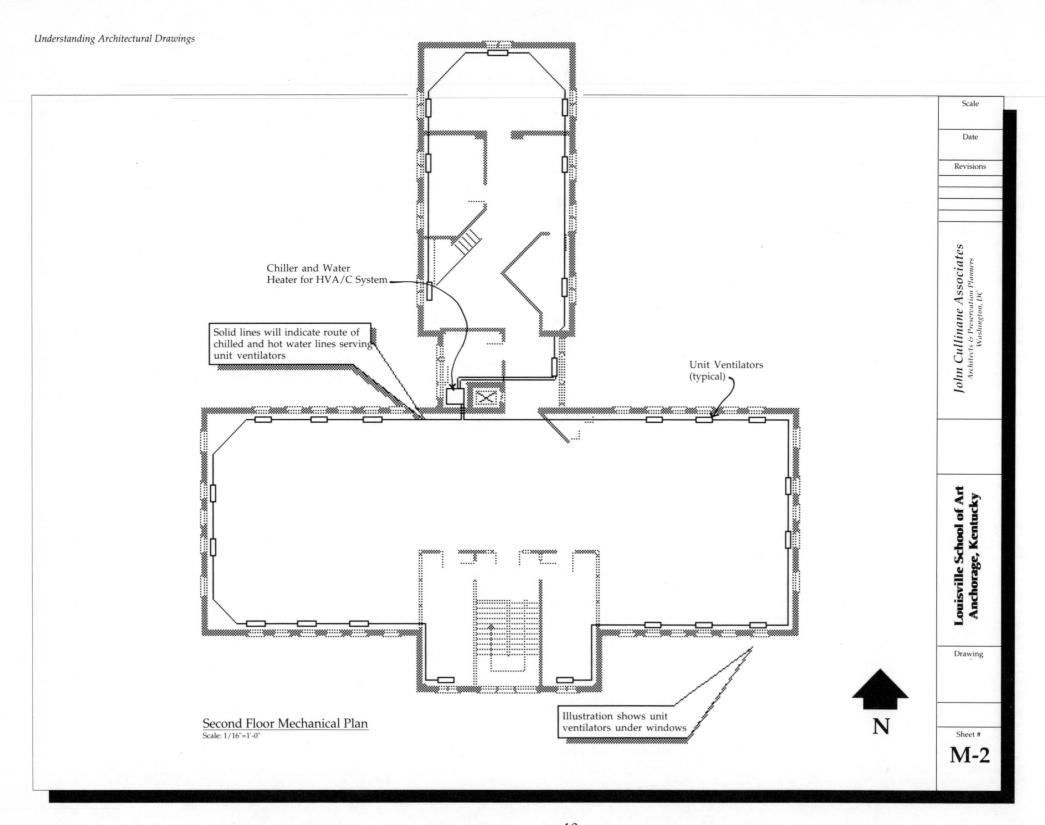

Chiller and Water
Heater for HVA/C System

Solid lines will indicate route of
chilled and hot water lines serving
unit ventilators

Unit Ventilators
(typical)

Illustration shows unit
ventilators under windows

Second Floor Mechanical Plan
Scale: 1/16"=1'-0"

N

Scale

Date

Revisions

John Cullinane Associates
Architects & Preservation Planners
Washington, DC

Louisville School of Art
Anchorage, Kentucky

Drawing

Sheet #

M-2

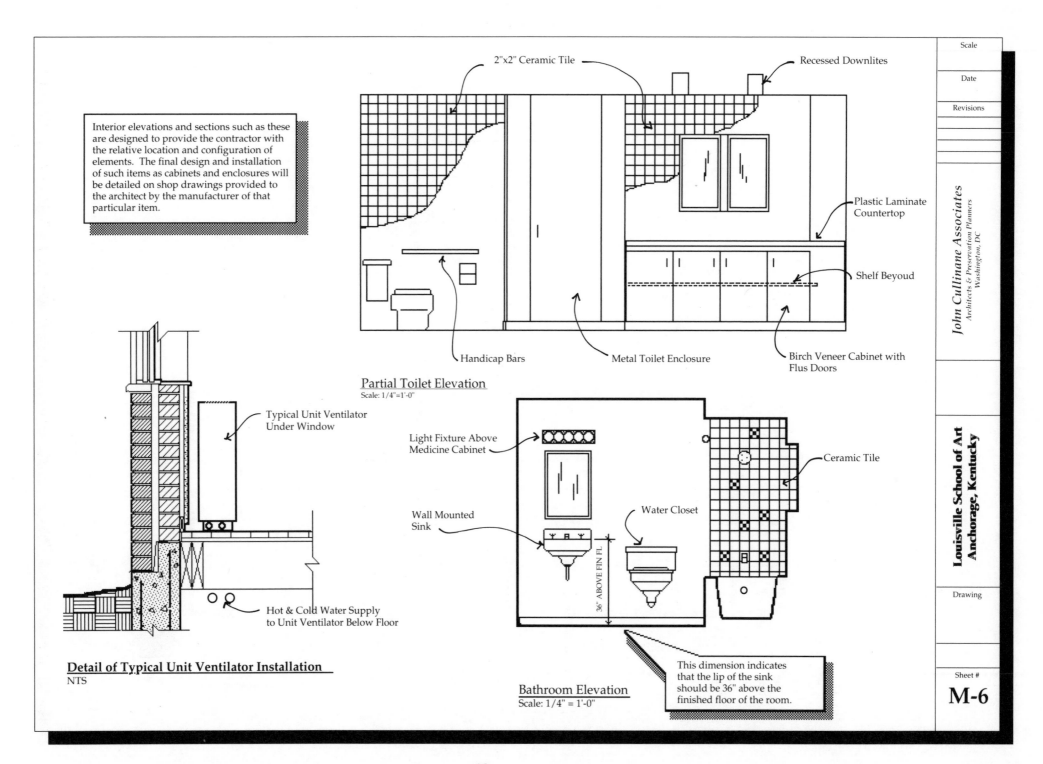

Interior elevations and sections such as these are designed to provide the contractor with the relative location and configuration of elements. The final design and installation of such items as cabinets and enclosures will be detailed on shop drawings provided to the architect by the manufacturer of that particular item.

2"x2" Ceramic Tile

Recessed Downlites

Plastic Laminate Countertop

Shelf Beyoud

Handicap Bars

Metal Toilet Enclosure

Birch Veneer Cabinet with Flus Doors

Partial Toilet Elevation
Scale: 1/4"=1'-0"

Typical Unit Ventilator Under Window

Light Fixture Above Medicine Cabinet

Ceramic Tile

Water Closet

Wall Mounted Sink

36" ABOVE FIN FL.

Hot & Cold Water Supply to Unit Ventilator Below Floor

Detail of Typical Unit Ventilator Installation
NTS

This dimension indicates that the lip of the sink should be 36" above the finished floor of the room.

Bathroom Elevation
Scale: 1/4" = 1'-0"

John Cullinane Associates
Architects & Preservation Planners
Washington, DC

Louisville School of Art
Anchorage, Kentucky

Scale

Date

Revisions

Drawing

Sheet #

M-6

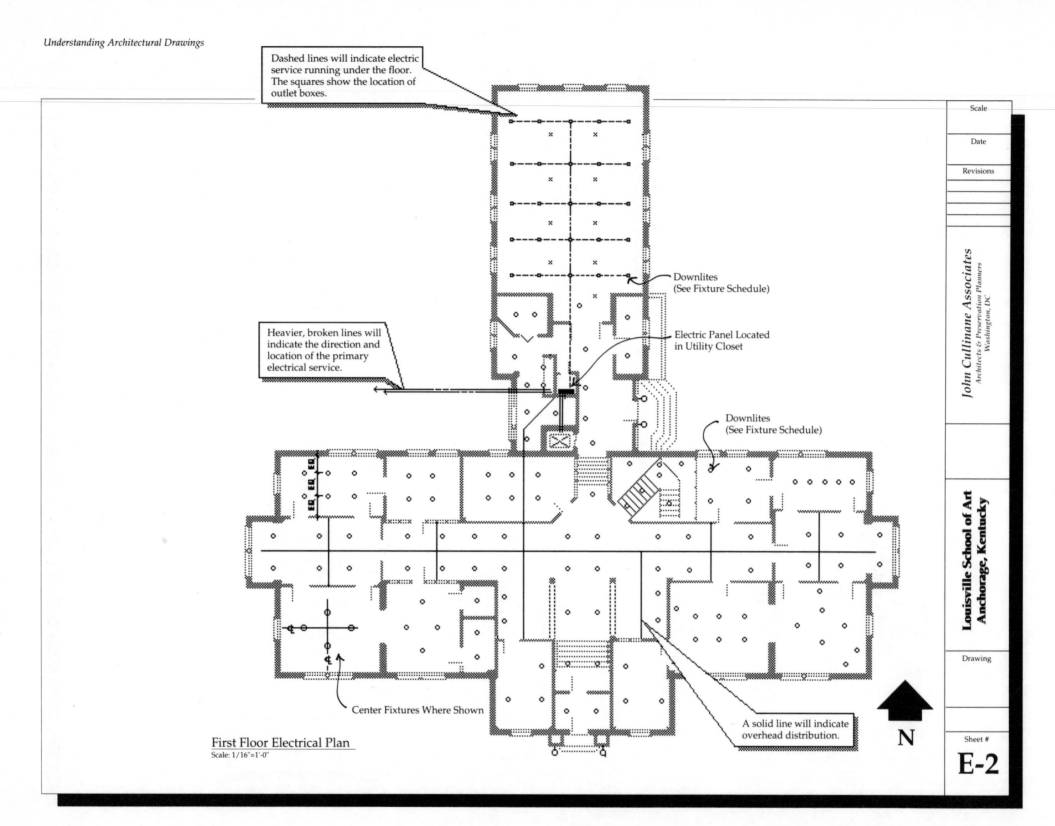

Dashed lines will indicate electric service running under the floor. The squares show the location of outlet boxes.

Downlites (See Fixture Schedule)

Heavier, broken lines will indicate the direction and location of the primary electrical service.

Electric Panel Located in Utility Closet

Downlites (See Fixture Schedule)

Center Fixtures Where Shown

A solid line will indicate overhead distribution.

First Floor Electrical Plan
Scale: 1/16"=1'-0"

Scale

Date

Revisions

John Cullinane Associates
Architects & Preservation Planners
Washington, DC

Louisville School of Art
Anchorage, Kentucky

Drawing

Sheet #

E-2

N

The proper installation of electrical service and equipment in a building or on a site relies heavily on the skills and expertise of contractors and workers. In addition, code restrictions on electrical service is usually very strict and explicit, dictating quantity of service, weight of electrical, and type of conduit, among other things. Consequently, electrical plans appear rather schematic in nature, and void of detail. Specifications for electrical service are similar, identifying materials and types, with less emphasis on execution than architectural or structural specs.

Usually the plans simply show the location of switches, lights, and outlets, allowing the electrical subcontractor to determine the most efficient way to deliver power to those locations. Lighting fixtures, whether interior or exterior, are identified by type, usually with a letter designation. These refer to a lighting schedule, either on the plans or in the specifications.

Even though electrical plans generally use architectural floor plans as a base, looking down from five feet above the floor, they will show switches, outlets, and fixtures from the floor to the ceiling. So the designations you see on a plan represent the electrical service in that space, not on the floor below or the floor above, as is the case with structural drawings. Also, convention and code requirements dictate the height and spacing of many electrical elements; accordingly, there will be no explicit details or indication of those locations. Occasionally, when a special service is provided, or a unique design, the exact location will be identified.

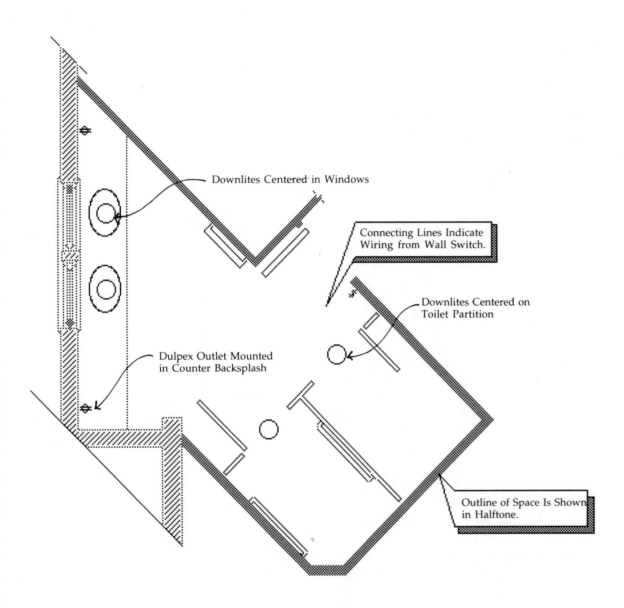

Downlites Centered in Windows

Connecting Lines Indicate
Wiring from Wall Switch.

Downlites Centered on
Toilet Partition

Dulpex Outlet Mounted
in Counter Backsplash

Outline of Space Is Shown
in Halftone.

Toilet Electrical Plan
Scale: 1/4" = 1'-0"

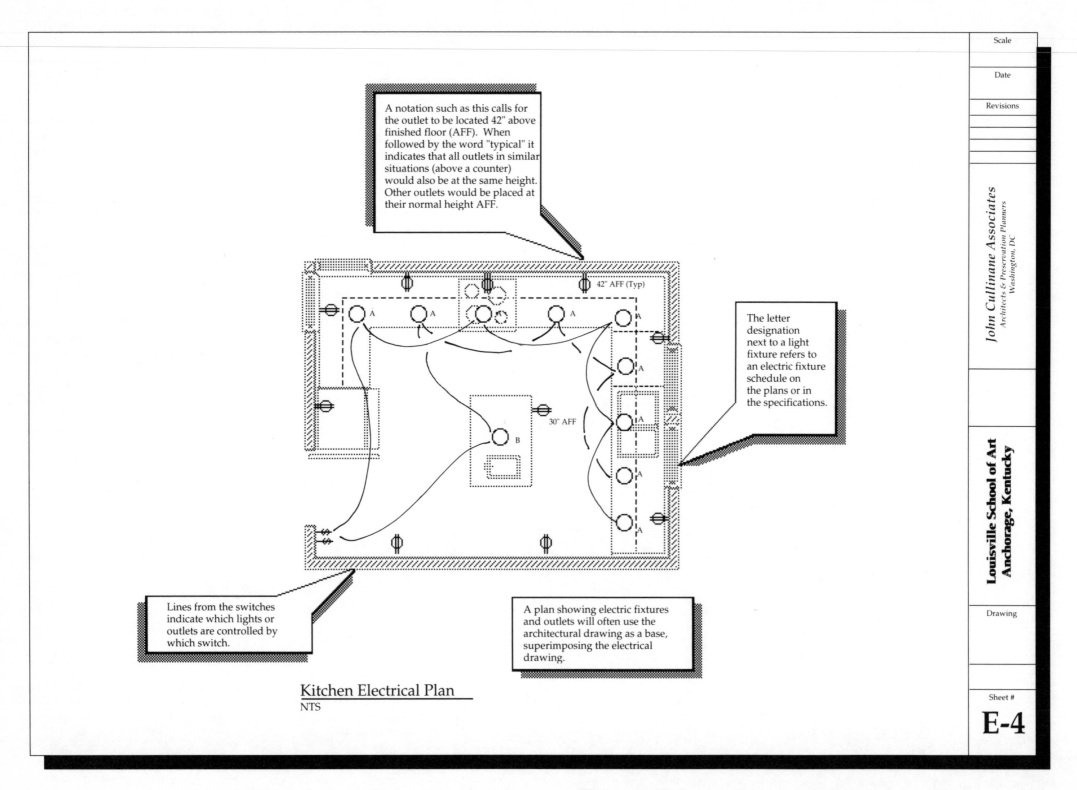

A notation such as this calls for the outlet to be located 42" above finished floor (AFF). When followed by the word "typical" it indicates that all outlets in similar situations (above a counter) would also be at the same height. Other outlets would be placed at their normal height AFF.

42" AFF (Typ)

The letter designation next to a light fixture refers to an electric fixture schedule on the plans or in the specifications.

30" AFF

Lines from the switches indicate which lights or outlets are controlled by which switch.

A plan showing electric fixtures and outlets will often use the architectural drawing as a base, superimposing the electrical drawing.

Kitchen Electrical Plan
NTS

Scale

Date

Revisions

John Cullinane Associates
Architects & Preservation Planners
Washington, DC

Louisville School of Art
Anchorage, Kentucky

Drawing

Sheet #

E-4

A significant component in any new design or rehabilitation is provision for the safety of occupants in case of fire. Every national and local building code requires protection of building users. The level of consideration varies according to the jurisdiction in which the building is located, the use of the structure, its type of construction, design, and condition.

In the 19th century, fire protection emphasized the preservation of property. Starting in the early 20th century, this emphasis shifted to the protection of human life. A fire-protection system in a building today includes such things as fire-rated exit doors, all swinging in the direction of the exit; fire-rated, noncombustible building materials used in exitways; construction and finish materials with controlled flame spread throughout the building; alarm systems, both visual and audible; fire stairs; sprinkler systems; and possibly "safe rooms" for use by handicapped occupants.

Fire-safety requirements in most building and fire codes are very specific. In many instances in historic buildings, strict adherence to fire-code requirements cannot be accomplished without damaging the character of that structure. Recognizing this problem, every national building code included provisions for waiver of strict code requirements in historic buildings if adequate alternative protective measures are taken. An example of this would be a situation where a historic open stairway would normally have to be closed, but the fire code and local fire marshall have allowed the stair to remain open if a sprinkler system is installed throughout the building.

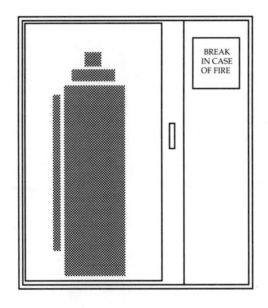

BREAK IN CASE OF FIRE

Typical Recessed Fire Box

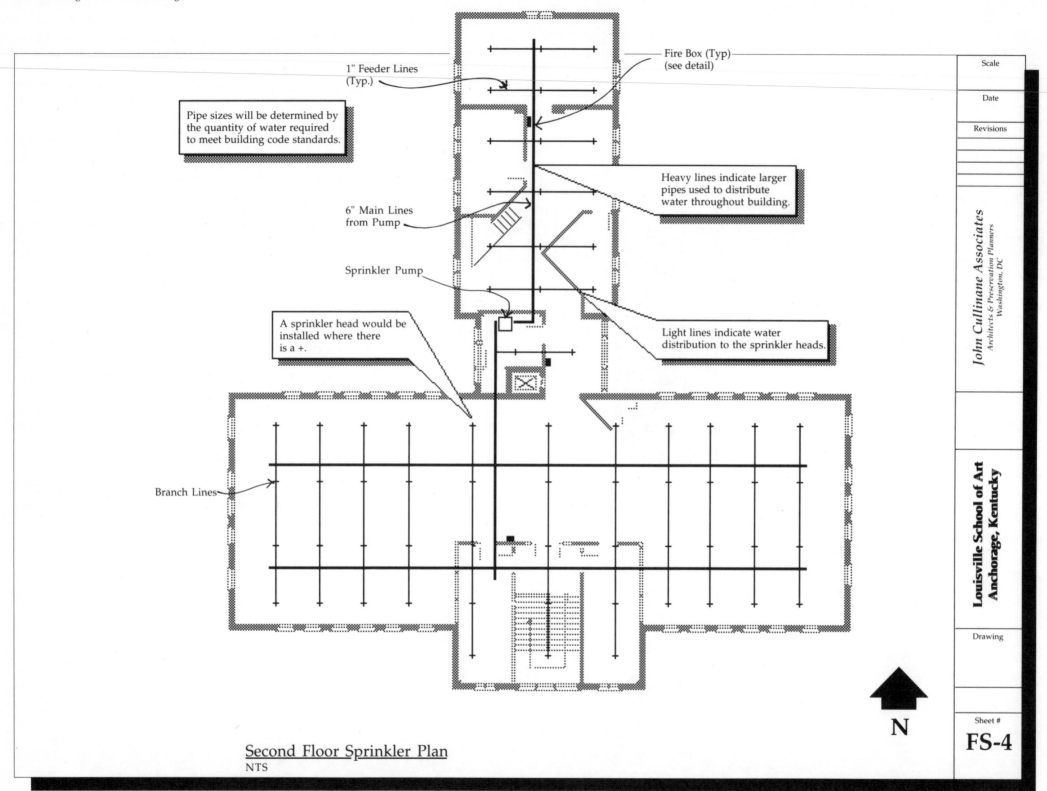

1" Feeder Lines
(Typ.)

Fire Box (Typ)
(see detail)

Pipe sizes will be determined by
the quantity of water required
to meet building code standards.

Heavy lines indicate larger
pipes used to distribute
water throughout building.

6" Main Lines
from Pump

Sprinkler Pump

A sprinkler head would be
installed where there
is a +.

Light lines indicate water
distribution to the sprinkler heads.

Branch Lines

John Cullinane Associates
Architects & Preservation Planners
Washington, DC

Louisville School of Art
Anchorage, Kentucky

Scale

Date

Revisions

Drawing

Sheet #

FS-4

N

Second Floor Sprinkler Plan
NTS

Construction specifications are more than the verbal equivalent of working drawings. They go beyond simply identifying the type and brand of material to be used. Where drawings indicate the location and form of elements, specifications are a multilayered set of instructions detailing the scope of work, quality of materials, standards of performance, and execution of work, along with testing and reporting requirements.

Specifications have evolved over many years in both content and method of development. In architecture and engineering offices, writing specs has historically been considered just about the least glamorous of jobs. However, their importance in ensuring a properly executed project, and the legal implications of issuing incorrect or incomplete specs, dictate that extreme care be taken in their development. On the job, and in the courts, instructions given in the specifications supersede those found on drawings. Consequently, architects go almost to extremes to prevent contradictions between these two sets of documents. Since the introduction of standardized formatting and computers, conflicts are less frequent, but still possible.

Architects formerly used a method of writing specifications called "cut and paste." This was exactly what it sounds like. An old specification that worked well would be pulled off of the shelf; and the spec writer, equipped with a pair of scissors and some glue, would attempt to edit the text to fit the new project. This system easily led to the inadvertent inclusion of materials and products not appropriate to a project which had been quite suitable for another project. Confusion would abound until addenda correcting the specifications were issued. Slowly, as word processors and computers were introduced into the office, this became less of a problem.

Also, the traditional method of developing new specs was for architects and engineers to obtain information on products or materials from manufacturers and simply specify those particular products. This did not always result in the least-expensive solution, especially if there were similar products that met the same functional and aesthetic criteria as those specified. Out of this problem first developed the phrase "or equal," or "or approved equal." This allowed the architect to specify a particular product, thus establishing a standard for function and appearance, but still permitted the contractor to recommend a less-expensive substitute. This, as you might imagine, could lead to terrible conflicts over whether a substitute was, in fact, equal to the original specified. In part to address this situation, "performance specifications" were developed. As the name implies, rather than calling for a particular product, these specs established a performance standard. Any product that met the standard would be acceptable, regardless of manufacturer. Some of the standards cited in performance specifications are established by testing laboratories and organizations, such as the American Society for Testing and Materials (ASTM); others are developed by the architect around a product that he or she knows would be acceptable. Most contemporary specifications are a combination of performance and product (or-approved-equal) specs.

The development of a consistent format for specifications has been a long process. The first problem was developing common nomenclature for construction activities. A universal set of categories of work was accepted when the Construction Specification Institute (CSI) created a uniform format. This divided construction activities into 16 major divisions, with each division subdivided into many sections. In addition, each section of specification is divided into three parts:

Part 1 -- General: Information on related
                      documents, such as drawings

                      Scope of work included in that
                      section

                      Performance requirements and
                      standards

                      Submittals required of the
                      contractor, such as shop
                      drawings or samples

                      Project conditions (usually
                      requiring the contractor to
                      undertake field measurements
                      prior to undertaking work or
                      ordering materials)

                      Warranties

Part 2 -- Products: Acceptable manufacturers
                      Materials
                      Fabrication
                      Finishes

Part 3 -- Execution: Inspections
                      Installation
                      Cleaning
                      Protection

The American Institute of Architects has taken the CSI format and refined the process of writing specifications into a fine art. Through its MASTERSPEC® system, the AIA provides both architects and engineers with computerized, preformatted, performance or product specifications ready for editing. All of the material and functional research that is so often not available to architects has been done by the MASTERSPEC® writers, allowing professionals to use it and be confident that the materials specified will meet their requirements. During this process, MASTERSPEC® has maintained the CSI nomenclature and formatting.

The division separations are self-explanatory, as are the subsections. No one project would ever use all of the specification sections. The architect and engineer will use just those portions that relate to their particular need.

Following are reprinted the titles of the MASTERSPEC® divisions and sections:

Division 1 -- General Requirements

01010	Summary of Work
01011	Summary of Work - Multiple
01020	Allowances
01026	Unit Prices
01027	Application for Payment
01030	Alternatives
01035	Modification Procedures
01040	Project Coordination
01041	Project Coordination - Multiple Projects
01045	Cutting and Patching
01050	Field Engineering
01095	Reference Standards and Definitions
01200	Project Meeting
01300	Submittals
01310	Schedules & Reports
01315	CPM Schedules & Reports
01340	Shop Drawings, Product Data & Samples
01380	Construction Photographs
01400	Quality Control Services
01500	Temporary Facilities
01501	Temporary Facilities - Multiple Prime Contracts
01600	Material and Equipment
01631	Product Substitutions
01700	Project Closeout
01710	Final Cleaning
01720	Project Record Documents
01730	Operating & Maintenance Data
01740	Warranties and Bonds

Division

Section

Part 1-General

Part 2-Products

Part 3-Execution

Division 2 -- Site Work

02060	Building Demolition
02070	Selective Demolition
02110	Site Clearing
02122	Tree Protection and Trimming
02140	Dewatering
02150	Shoring and Bracing
02200	Earthwork
02282	Termite Control
02360	Driven Piles
02380	Caissons
02511	Hot-mixed Asphalt Paving
02515	Unit Pavers
02520	Portland Cement Conc. Paving
02668	Water Service Piping
02669	Private Fire Service Mains
02670	Water Wells
02710	Foundation Drainage
02720	Storm Sewerage
02730	Sanitary Sewerage
02740	Septic Systems
02776	Pond & Reservoir Liners
02810	Underground Irrigation System
02813	Chain Link Fences & Gates
02900	Landscape Work
02930	Lawns and Grasses
02955	Trees and Shrubs
02956	Ground Cover and Plants

Division 3 -- Concrete

03300	Cast-in-Place Concrete
03320	Concrete Floor Topping
03355	Special Concrete Finishes
03361	Shotcrete
03410	Structural Precast Concrete
03411	Precast Prestressed Hollow Core Slabs
03412	Precast Prestressed Long-span Units
03413	Precast Prestressed Structural Framing Units
03450	Architectural Precast Concrete -plant Cast
03455	Glass Fiber Reinforced Precast Conc. - Plant Cast
03470	Tilt-up Concrete Construction
03520	Insulating Concrete Decks
03531	Cementitious Wood Fiber Planks

Division 4 -- Masonry

04200	Unit Masonry
04241	Structural Clay Facing Units
04270	Glass Unit Masonry
04405	Dimension Stone
04450	Stone Tile
04500	Masonry Restoration & Cleaning

Division 5 -- Metals

05210	Structural Steel
05220	Steel Joists & Joist Girders
05310	Steel Deck
05400	Cold-formed Metal Framing
05500	Metal Fabrications
05521	Pipe & Tube Railings
05580	Sheet Metal Fabrications
05700	Ornamental Metalwork
05715	Prefabricated Spiral Stairs
05720	Ornamental Handrails & Railings
05810	Expansion Joint Cover Assemblies

Division 6 -- Wood and Plastic

06100	Rough Carpentry
06130	Heavy Timber Construction
06170	Structural Glued Laminated Units
06192	Prefabricated Metal-Plate-Connected Wood Trusses
06200	Finish Carpentry
06265	Molded Archit. Ornamentation
06401	Exterior Archit. Woodwork
06402	Interior Archit. Woodwork
06410	Custom Casework
06420	Panelwork

Division 7 -- Thermal and Moisture Protection

07110	Sheet Membrane Waterproofing
07120	Fluid-applied Waterproofing
07125	Sheet Metal Waterproofing
07130	Bentonite Waterproofing
07140	Metal Oxide Waterproofing
07160	Bituminous Dampproofing
07175	Water Repellents
07210	Building Insulation
07241	Exterior Insulation & Finish Systems-class PB
07242	Exterior Insulation & Finish System-class PM
07250	Sprayed-on Fireproofing
07266	Mineral Fiber Board
07311	Asphalt Shingles
07313	Metal Shingles
07315	Slate Shingles
07317	Wood Shingles & Shakes
07320	Roof Tiles
07410	Manufactured Roof and Wall Paels
07411	Manufactured Roof Panels
07412	Manufactured Wall Panels
07460	Siding
07511	Built-up Asphalt Roofing
07512	Built-up Coal Tar Roofing
07530	Single Ply Membrane Roofing
07540	Fluid-applied Roofing
07570	Traffic Topping
07600	Flashing and Sheet Metal
07610	Sheet Metal Roofing
07700	Roof Specialties & Accessories
07710	Manufactured Roof Specialties
07716	Roof Expansion Assemblies
07820	Metal-framed Skylights
07900	Joint Sealers

Division 8 -- Doors and Windows

08111	Standard Steel Doors & Frames
08114	Custom Steel Doors & Frames
08211	Flush Wood Doors
08212	Panel Wood Doors
08305	Access Doors
08311	Alum. Sliding Glass Doors
08312	Wood Sliding Glass Doors
08314	Sliding Metal Fire Doors
08318	Insulating Security Doors
08330	Overhead Coiling Doors
08340	Overhead Coiling Grills
08351	Folding Doors
08360	Sectional Overhead Doors
08390	Screen and Storm Doors
08410	Alum. Entrances & Storefronts
08450	All-glass Entrances
08460	Automatic Entrance Doors
08470	Revolving Doors
08510	Steel Windows
08520	Aluminum Windows
08525	Alum. Architectural Windows
08560	Aluminum Storm Windows
08610	Wood Windows
08710	Finish Hardware
08720	Door Operators
08800	Glass & Glazing
08825	Decorative Glass
08830	Mirrored Glass
08840	Plastic Glazing
08920	Glazed Alum. Curtain Walls
08925	Structural Sealant Glazed CutainWall
08960	Sloped Glazing Systems

Division 9 -- Finishes

09200	Lath & Plaster
09206	Metal Lath & Furring
09215	Veneer Plaster
09220	Portland Cement Plaster
09250	Gypsum Drywall
09261	Predecorated Gypsum Board
09262	Gypsum Sheathing
09270	Gypsum Bd. Shaft Wall Systems
09300	Tile
09400	Terrazzo
09511	Acoustical Panel Ceilings
09512	Acoustical Tile Ceilings
09513	Acoustical Snap-in Metal Pan Ceilings
09521	Acoustical Wall Panels
09546	Linear Metal Ceilings
09549	Suspended Decorative Grids
09550	Wood Flooring
09563	Wood Athletic Flooring
09565	Wood Block Flooring
09600	Interior Stonework
09635	Brick Flooring
09636	Chemical-resistant Brick Flooring
09650	Resilient Flooring
09660	Resilient Tile Flooring
09664	Rubber Tile Flooring
09665	Resilient Sheet Flooring
09670	Fluid-applied Resilient Flooring
09675	Conductive Resilient Flooring
09678	Resilient Base and Accessories
09780	Carpet
09690	Carpet Tile
09705	Resinous Flooring
09800	Special Coatings
09830	Elastomeric Coatings
09841	Fire Retardant Coatings
09900	Painting
09931	Exterior Wood Stains
09950	Wall Coverings
09961	Vinyl Wallcovering
09970	Wallpaper
09975	Textile Wallcovering
09976	Heavy Duty Synthetic Textile Wallcovering
09980	Wood Veneer Wallcovering

Division 10 -- Specialties

10100	Visual Display Boards
10160	Toilet Partitions
10180	Stone Toilet Partitions
10191	Cubicle Curtains & Track
10200	Louvers & Vents
10250	Service Wall Systems
10260	Wall & Corner Guards
10270	Access Flooring
10350	Flagpoles
10416	Directories & Bulletin Boards
10425	Signs
10436	Exterior Port & Panel Signs
10437	Exterior Pylon Signs
10500	Metal Lockers
10522	Fire Extingushers, Cabinets and Accessories
10550	Postal Specialties
10605	Wire Mesh Partitions
10615	Demountable Partitions
10616	Demountable Aluminum Framed Partitions
10617	Demountable Gypsum Panel Partitions
10618	Demountable Metal Partitions
10652	Folding Panel Partitions
10653	Fire-rated Folding Panel Partitions
10655	Accordion Folding Partitions
10675	Metal Storage Shelving
10681	High Density Storage & Shelving
10750	Telephone Specialties
10753	Wall-mounted Telephone Enclosures
10800	Toilet & Bath Accessories

Division 11 -- Equipment

11030	Teller & Service Equipment
11050	Library Equipment
11054	Library Stack System
11060	Portable Theater & Stage Equip.
11062	Stage Curtains
11100	Mercantile Equipment
11132	Projection Screens
11150	Parking Control Equipment
11160	Loading Dock Equipment
11170	Solid Waste Handling Equipment
11306	Packaged Pump Stations
11400	Food Service Equipment
11450	Residential Equipment
11460	Unit Kitchens
11610	Laboratory Fume Hoods
11910	Mailroom Equip. & Furniture

Division 12 -- Furnishings

12052	Upholstery Fabrics
12320	Restaurant & Cafeteria Casework
12345	Laboratory Casework
12372	Kitchen Casework
12500	Window Treatment
12511	Vertical Louver Blinds
12512	Horizontal Louver Blinds
12520	Shades
12530	Window Treatment Hardware
12540	Draperies & Curtains
12611	Systems Furniture
12620	Furniture
12625	Hospital Furniture
12630	Restaurant Furniture
12631	Metal Casegoods
12632	Wood & Laminate Casegoods
12676	Custom Rugs
12680	Foot Grilles
12690	Floor Mats and Frames
12700	Multiple Seating
12710	Auditorium & Treater Seating
12760	Telescoping Bleachers
12800	Interior Plants & Planters
12900	Building Accessories

Division 13 -- Special Construction

13052	Saunas
13091	X-ray Projection
13122	Metal Building Systems
13610	Solar Flat Plate Collectors
13810	Energy Monitoring & Control Systems

Division 14 -- Conveying Systems

14100	Dumbwaiters
14210	Electric Traction Elevators
14240	Hydraulic Elevators
14310	Escalators
14320	Moving Walks
14420	Wheelchair Lifts
14560	Chutes

Division 15 -- Mechanical

15010	Basic Mechanical Requirements
15030	Electrical Requirement for Mechanical Equip.
15050	Basic Mechanical Materials and Methods
15055	Basic Piping Materials & Methods
15100	Valves
15125	Pipe Expansion Joints
15135	Meters & Gages
15140	Support & Anchors
15190	Mechanical Identification
15241	Vibration Control
15250	Mechanical Insulation
15300	Fire Protection
15320	Fire Pumps
15411	Water Distribution Piping
15412	Sanitary Drainage & Vent Systems
15413	Storm Drainage Systems
15420	Drainage & Vent Systems
15440	Plumbing Fixtures
15453	Plumbing Pumps
15455	Storage Tanks
15457	Water Softeners
15459	Interceptors
15460	Water Heaters
15481	Compressed Air Systems
15483	Fuel Oil Systems

15485	Medical Gas Systems
15488	Natural Gas Systems
15493	Laboratory Drainage Systems
15494	Laboratory Supply Systems
15510	Hydronic Piping
15520	Steam & Condensate Piping
15526	Condensate Pump & Receiver Sets
15530	Refrigerant Piping
15540	HVAC Pumps
15556	Cast-iron Boilers
15557	Scotch Marine Boilers
15558	Electric Boilers
15561	Firebox Boilers
15562	Pulse Combustion Boilers
15570	Boiler Accessories
15575	Breechings, Chimneys, & Stacks
15580	Feedwater Equipment
15585	Deaerators
15586	Boiler Water Treatment Systems
15620	Fuel-fired Heaters
15670	Condensing Units
15681	Absorption Chillers
15683	Reciprocation Chillers
15685	Centrifugal Chillers-Water Cooled
15686	Centrifugal Chillers-Air Cooled
15711	Factory-Fabricated Cooling Towers
15713	Ejector Cooling Towers
15730	Liquid Coolers
15742	Evaporative Condensers
15743	Air-cooled Condensers
15749	Condenser Water Treatment Systems
15755	Heat Exchangers
15781	Packaged Heating & Cooling Units
15782	Rooftop Heating & Cooling Units
15786	Water Source Heat Pumps
15810	Humidifiers
15830	Heating Terminal Units
15845	Energy Recovery Units
15850	Air Handling
15854	Central-Station Air-Handling Units
15860	Centrifugal Fans
15865	Axial Fans
15870	Power Ventilators
15885	Air Cleaning
15891	Metal Ductwork

15893	Nonmetal Ductwork
15895	HVAC Casings
15910	Ductwork Accessories
15920	Sound Attenuators
15932	Air Outlets & Inlets
15933	Air Terminals
15971	Electric Control Systems
15973	Pneumatic Control Systems
15985	Sequence of Operation
15990	Testing, Adjusting, & Balancing

Division 16 -- Electrical

16010	Basic Electrical Requirements
16050	Basic Electrical Materials & Methods
16110	Raceways
16111	Cable Trays
16118	Underfloor Ducts
16119	Underground Ducts & Manholes
16120	Wire & Cables
16121	Control/Signal Transmission Media
16122	Undercarpet Cabling Systems
16123	Optical Fiber Cabling Systems
16124	Medium-voltage Cable
16135	Electrical Boxes & Fittings
16143	Wiring Devices
16170	Circuit & Motor Disconnects
16190	Supporting Devices
16195	Electrical Identification
16312	Secondary Unit Substations
16320	Medium-voltage Transformers
16344	Medium-voltage Switchgear
16410	Power Factor Correction
16420	Service Entrance
16425	Switchboards
16426	Low-voltage Power Switchgear
16438	Rectifiers & Inverters
16452	Grounding
16460	Transformers
16466	Busways
16470	Panelboards
16475	Overcurrent Protective Devices
16477	Fuses
16481	Motor Controllers
16482	Motor-control Centers
16495	Transfer Switches
16503	Poles & Standards
16512	Exterior Lighting Fixtures
16515	Interior Lighting Fixtures

16535	Emergency Lighting
16551	Roadway & Parking Area Lighting
16580	Theatrical Lighting
16610	Uninterruptible Power Supply Systems.
16621	Diesel Generator Systems
16631	Central Battery Systems
16660	Ground-fault Protection System
16670	Lightning Protection Systems
16721	Fire Alarm Systems
16730	Clock & Program Systems
16740	Telephone Systems
16750	Nurses Call Systems
16760	Intercommunication Systems
16770	Public Address Systems
16775	Sound Masking System
16780	Television Systems
16781	Master Antenna TV Systems
16782	Closed-circuit TV Systems
16783	Satellite Earth Station Systems
16790	Broadband Local Area Network System
16802	Electric Radiant Ceiling Panels
16851	Electric Heating Terminals
16856	Electric Heating Cables
16860	Electric Duct Heaters
16875	Electric Unit Ventilators
16880	Electric Radiant Heaters
16931	Lighting Control Equipment

Every structure is made up of a series of interdependent systems. Like a house of cards, each is supported on another--together forming a complete structure. When reading plans and specifications for new construction, or reviewing rehabilitation work on an existing building, it is important to identify and understand the individual systems and how they contribute to the overall project.

The primary building systems are: Structural--including foundations and framing; Mechanical--including heating, ventilating, air conditioning, and plumbing; and Electrical.

Structural System

One of the critical building systems, the structural system is made up of the basic supporting elements of the building--the foundations and the framing.

In any structure or building, the first and most important system is the foundation. It is the base on which the remainder of the building is constructed. A foundation system will consist of almost everything below grade, such as piling, footings, foundation walls, and grade beams. Once they are in place, their configuration and dimension generally establish the form and size of the building. With the exception of some specialized designs, a building extends up from the edge of the foundation. Also, the anticipated weight and loading of the building would have determined the size of the foundation components, such as footings. Consequently, once the foundation is in, a building of a larger size, weight, or loading could not be constructed without supplementing the foundation.

The second component of the overall structural system is the framing. This term refers to all of the components above grade level that are required to support the building. That would include floor and roof joists, trusses, or beams; exterior and interior wall construction required to support the floor and roof framing; subfloors and roof sheathing; and, in the case of concrete construction, floor slabs. All other wall framing and floor and roof construction within a building are nonstructural, that is, if they were removed the structure or building would remain standing.

Mechanical System

Mechanical systems within a building include the heating, ventilating system, air-conditioning system, and plumbing. The heating, ventilating, and air conditioning will simply be referred to as the HV A/C system. As the letters indicate, it is generally an integrated system, rather than three separate systems. However, in some specialized designs or situations, the three will be designed and installed separately. In all cases, the HV A/C system is designed to take outside air into the building, filter it, either heat or cool it, and distribute that conditioned air throughout the structure. Once distributed, the system then circulates the air and either exhausts or recycles it.

The plumbing system includes bringing water and other fluids or gases into the building, distributing them to spaces for specific uses -- such as in kitchens or bathrooms -- venting gases, and disposing of waste. Plumbing would also include the treatment of water, such as filtering, heating, and cooling, and the water supply and drain lines for fire-sprinkler systems within a structure.

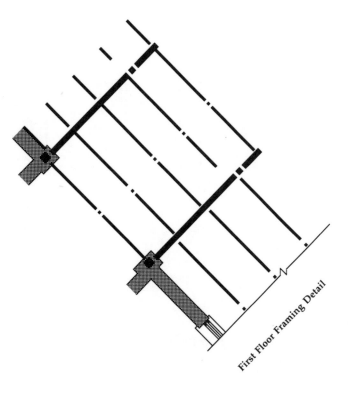

First Floor Framing Detail

Electrical System

Another major system in a building is the electrical. This includes the electric power coming into the building and its distribution. Electrical systems can be simple, such as power coming into a single distribution box and then wires extending through the structure to power fixtures, switches, and outlets, or it can be very complex. But regardless of the size and complexity of the system, its purpose is to provide controlled electric power for specific and general needs on demand.

Other Systems

In addition to the three primary building systems, there are systems involving doors and windows, security, fire protection, and vertical transportation (stairs, ramps, escalators, and elevators).

Separate from these would be numerous other systems required to make a structure function properly. These include moisture protection -- incorporating foundation dampproofing, flashing, weatherstripping, vapor barriers, and roofing systems; energy conservation -- including foundation wall, exterior wall, ceiling, and roof insulation, insulating door and window systems, and possibly passive and active solar energy systems; acoustics -- comprising sound retarding and enhancing systems, sound insulation and isolation systems; wall construction and architectural finishes -- exterior (non-structural) materials, interior floor, wall and ceiling systems; and, coatings -- including clear and tinted (paint or stain) coatings.

It all sounds complicated; but when each system is integrated into the design, the result is a building that functions as it was intended to, while the complexity of the systems is not apparent to the user -- perhaps like a good computer program.

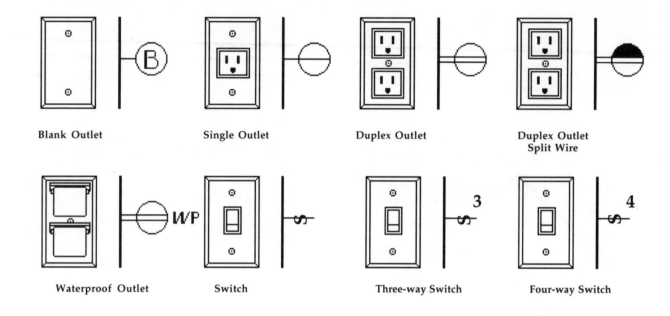

Blank Outlet	Single Outlet	Duplex Outlet	Duplex Outlet Split Wire

Waterproof Outlet	Switch	Three-way Switch	Four-way Switch

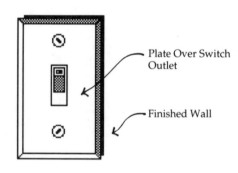

Plate Over Switch Outlet

Finished Wall

Escutcheon

One of the most important elements in the definition of any building is the treatment of the fenestration, specifically the doors and windows. Although their primary functions are practical, and basic to the way buildings are used, their placement and design are often a reflection of the technology and style prevalent in the period in which the building was designed. Accordingly, when viewing the design and treatment of doors and windows, it is important to understand their contribution to the character of a building in order to evaluate the appropriateness of treatment.

Although the basic, functional design of doors and windows has remained almost unchanged over the centuries, their detailed design style, proportions, details, and glazing have changed considerably. These changes can readily be seen in the transition from early and late colonial periods of architectural style in the United States to the Adamesque and Federal periods, and then from Federal through the Victorian period into the early 20th century. Such changes involve the form and scale of window and door elements, such as muntins and fanlights, the size of glass panes, and the type of trim surrounding an opening. All of these elements speak to the technology available at the time of the design and construction of a building, and the architectural taste of the period. An example of this is the use of muntins in a window sash. Up until 1853 the primary method of creating window glass was blowing a glass cylinder, cutting it, and flattening it out into a pane of glass. Because of this method, the size of a window was dictated by the size of glass cylinder an individual could create. Thus, the use of wood elements (muntins) was necessary to connect many small panes of glass, making a large window sash. In 1853 a commercial method of floating glass was developed, allowing manufacturers to make glass sheets as large as desired. This is why you will normally see multipaned windows in buildings predating 1853, and larger windows in structures constructed after that date, at least up until the Colonial Revival period in the early 20th century.

When drawn on architectural plans and elevations, seldom will a fully accurate drawing of door or window elements be shown at a small scale. The small-scale drawings will usually show a reference number, letter, or symbol that refers to a door and window schedule and large-scale drawings. Also, the set of specifications will provide a detailed description of the materials and method of construction for these components. But even with all of this information in the contract documents, the final door and window design will be determined only after "shop drawings" are developed and submitted to the architect for review and approval.

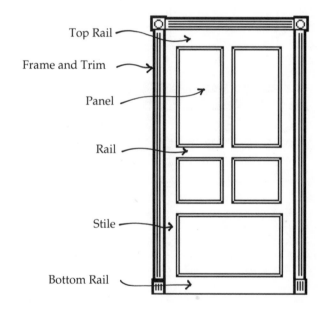

Anatomy of a Door

NTS

Window Schedule

#	Size	Type	Mat	Finish	Glazing	Remarks
101	3'-0" x 5'-6"	A	Wd	Paint	Tinted	Replace Sash Cords
102	6'-6" x 5'-6"	B	Wd	Paint	Tinted	See Spec for finish color
103	6'-6" x 5'-6"	B	Wd	Paint	Tinted	See Spec for finish color
104	3'-0" x 5'-6"	A	Wd	Stain	Clear	See Spec for finish color
105	3'-0" x 5'-6"	A	Wd	Stain	Clear	See Spec for finish color
106	3'-0" x 5'-6"	A	Wd	Stain	Clear	See Spec for finish color
107						
201	3'-0" x 5'-6"	A	Wd	Paint	Tinted	Replace Sash Cords
202	6'-6" x 5'-6"	B	Wd	Paint	Tinted	See Spec for finish color

Door Schedule

#	Size	Type	Mat	Finish	Const.	Remarks
001	3'-6"x6'-8"x1-1/2"	B	Wd	Painted	HC	
002	3'-6"x6'-8"x1-1/2"	C	Wd	Painted	HC	
003	3'-6"x6'-8"x1-1/2"	B	Wd	Painted	HC	
004	3'-6"x6'-8"x1-1/2"	B	Wd	Painted	HC	Undercut 1" for carpet
101	3'-6"x6'-8"x1-3/4"	A	Wd	Clear	SC	
102						
103						
104						
105						

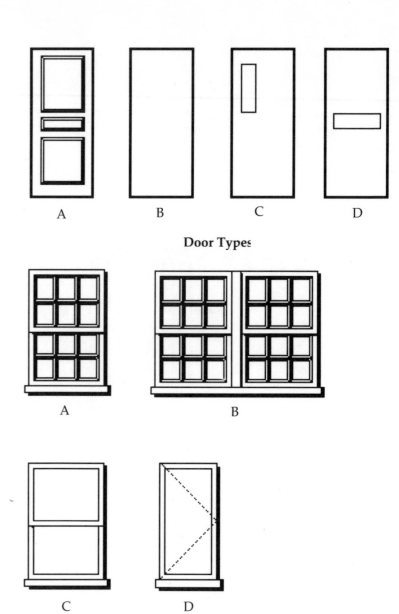

A   B   C   D

Door Types

A   B

C   D

Window Types

The door and window schedules will provide a complete list of all of those components found in the building. They will detail the size and material, and reference design types. More specific information, such as what constitutes a solid or hollow-core door, and how to apply a clear finish, would be found in the appropriate specifications section.

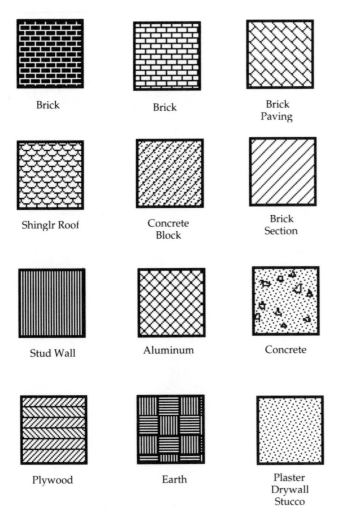

Brick

Brick

Brick
Paving

Shinglr Roof

Concrete
Block

Brick
Section

Stud Wall

Aluminum

Concrete

Plywood

Earth

Plaster
Drywall
Stucco

Building materials can vary greatly, depending on the building use, the type of construction, and the geographic location. Even on the same project, it would not be unusual to have hundreds of different materials used in various manners. Generally, there should be a logic to their use and how they relate to each other. An example of this would be the use of a stone foundation below a brick structure. Because the stone is viewed as a heavier and stronger material, its placement in a foundation is logical. The reverse situation, with the brick below and the stone above, would not appear rational, although it might have some architectural interest. Even the texture of a material will suggest an appropriate use. If stone is used on a project, a rough finish would be better used on the base and lower portions of a structure, while a smoother finish would work better higher up. Another example would be the use of wood below stone or brick. Because just about everyone would view masonry as heavier than wood, such an arrangement would appear very strange; but, again, it could provide some interesting designs.

Many materials and building techniques used extensively in construction during the 18th, 19th, and early 20th centuries are no longer available or popular today, such as cast iron and decorative plaster. Some basic materials, however, have remained constant, like wood and masonry. The species of wood and the manufacturing techniques for the brick may have changed, but the material and the method with which it is used has remained basically the same. In a historic structure it usually was fairly easy to identify the building materials. If it looked like stone, chances are that's what it was. There were some popular techniques used to simulate other types of material for decorative effects, such as marbleizing plaster and graining cheap wood doors to simulate a more expensive species; and in the Victorian period of design, pressed metal was often used in lieu of carved wood. But, generally, materials were used for their durability and texture. Stone looked like stone, brick like brick, and wood like wood.

New technology, however, has taken the simulation of building material and its use to new heights. In an effort to maintain the character and style of historic designs and buildings, material manufacturers have developed ever-more interesting adaptations of new technology. When viewing a new building with a stone base, you may find that the material is actually architectural concrete made to look like stone. Wood siding can be replaced by aluminum and vinyl, textured to look and feel like wood. Decorative detailing that once was made of carved wood or pressed metal can now be made of fiberglass.

Even in the design and assembly of this material there is a level of chicanery. Historically, windows were separated into small panes of glass because the technology of making glass limited the size of the pane, thus the use of muntins. Current technology allows the manufacture of just about any size piece of glass, eliminating the need for muntins. However, in the interest of design, many new buildings retain what appear to be window muntins. These, unfortunately, are usually vinyl strips glued to a large window pane. Another example of this is the system of using "preassembled" brick or stone panels in building construction. Rather than relying on the traditional techniques of placing masonry material in place piece by piece, some architects and contractors have found it more economical to assemble large panels of this material off-site, in a factory, and then just place them on the building with the use of a crane. It is important to notice these uses and applications of materials when reading a set of construction documents.

On a set of drawings, most materials have a unique symbol or texture, providing easy identification for the contractor. Reading and understanding these become almost second nature to those in the profession. Even though the symbols are standardized, there will usually be a "legend" of materials somewhere near the beginning of the set of drawings. This legend will illustrate the symbol or texture and then immediately identify it. By doing this, architects avoid misunderstandings over the construction materials to be used.

- ☑ Secretary of the Interior's Standards for Rehabilitation
- ☑ Secretary of the Interior's Guidelines for Rehabilitating Historic Buildings
- ☑ Americans with Disabilities Act
- ☑ BOCA Code
- ☐ Fire-Safety Standards
- ☐ State Historic Preservation Officer Review
- ☐ Advisory Council Review
- ☑ Landmarks Commission Review
- ☑ Architectural Review Board
- ☑ National Park Service: Preservation Briefs
- ☐ Energy Conservation
- ☐
- ☐
- ☐

Probably the most widely used standards for viewing architectural plans and assessing the treatment of existing buildings, and the design of new structures, is a set of guidelines developed and published by the secretary of the interior. Known as the Secretary of the Interior's Standards for Rehabilitation and Guidelines for Rehabilitating Historic Buildings, this guidance is used as the basis for all state and federal government reviews under tax-certification programs and is employed extensively by local landmarks commissions and review boards.

Under the National Historic Preservation Act passed in 1966, the secretary of the interior was responsible for establishing standards for all programs under the Department of the Interior authority and for advising federal agencies on the preservation of historic properties listed or eligible for listing in the National Register of Historic Places. In partial fulfillment of this responsibility, the Secretary of the Interior's Standards for Historic Preservation Projects were developed to direct work undertaken on historic buildings.

The Standards for Rehabilitation (Federal Code 36 CFR 67) comprise that section of the overall historic preservation project standards addressing rehabilitation. "Rehabilitation" is defined as the process of returning a property to a state of utility, through repair or alteration, which makes possible an efficient contemporary use while preserving those portions and features of the property which are significant to its historic, architectural, and cultural values.

As issued by the Department of the Interior, the Standards for Rehabilitation include a preamble that sets forth criteria for application of the Standards, and detailed guidelines for application.

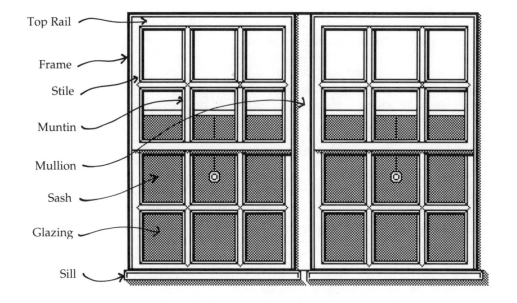

Top Rail

Frame

Stile

Muntin

Mullion

Sash

Glazing

Sill

Anatomy of a Window

NTS

The preamble reads as follows:

(a) The following Standards for Rehabilitation are the criteria used to determine if a rehabilitation project qualifies as a certified rehabilitation. The intent of the Standards is to assist the long-term preservation of a property's significance through the preservation of historic materials and features. The Standards pertain to historic buildings of all materials, construction types, sizes, and occupancy and encompass the exterior and interior of historic buildings. The Standards also encompass related landscape features, the building's site and environment, as well as attached, adjacent, or related new construction. To be certified, a rehabilitation project must be determined by the secretary to be consistent with the historic character of the structure(s) and, where applicable, the district in which it is located.

(b) The following Standards are to be applied to specific rehabilitation projects in a reasonable manner, taking into consideration economic and technical feasibility:

(1) Place a property in a use, either continuing or new, that requires minimal change to the defining characteristics of the historic building and its site and environment.

(2) Retain and preserve the historic character of a property. Avoid the removal of historic materials or alteration of features and spaces that characterize a property.

(3) Recognize each property as a physical record of its time, place, and use. Do not undertake changes that create a false sense of historical development, such as adding conjectural features or features from other properties.

(4) Retain and preserve those changes that have taken place in the course of time which are evidence of the property's development and which have acquired historical significance in their own right.

(5) Preserve distinctive features, finishes, and construction techniques or examples of craftsmanship that characterize a property.

(6) Repair rather than replace deteriorated historic features and their materials. Where the severity of deterioration requires replacement of a distinctive feature, match the historic feature in design, color, texture, and other visual qualities and, where possible, material. Substantiate replacement of missing features by documentary, physical, or pictorial evidence.

(7) Do not use chemical or physical treatments, such as sandblasting, that cause damage to historic materials. Undertake the surface cleaning of structures, if appropriate, using the gentlest means possible.

(8) Protect and preserve significant archeological resources affected by a project. If such resources must be disturbed, undertake mitigation measures.

(9) Do not destroy those historic materials that characterize the property and its environment when undertaking new additions, alterations, or related new construction. Differentiate new work from the old to protect the historic integrity of the property and respect its massing, size, scale, and architectural details.

(10) Undertake new additions and adjacent or related new construction in such a manner that if removed in the future, the essential form and integrity of the historic property and its environment are unimpaired.

The Secretary of the Interior's Guidelines for Rehabilitating Historic Buildings is an extensive description of the methods of applying the 10 Standards. The guidelines address major building systems and design concerns, detailing "recommended" and "not recommended" actions in every instance. They are formatted in a manner that first addresses the preservation and rehabilitation of building elements, then the design for missing historic features, then alterations and additions for the new use.

The guideline categories are:

Building Exterior
   Masonry: Brick, stone, terra cotta, concrete, adobe, stucco, and mortar
   Wood: Clapboard, weatherboard, shingles, and other wooden siding and decorative elements
   Architectural Metals: Cast iron, steel, pressed tin, copper, aluminum, and zinc
   Roofs
   Windows
   Entrances and Porches
   Storefronts
Building Interior
   Structural Systems
   Spaces, Features, Finishes
   Mechanical Systems
Building Site
Setting: District or Neighborhood
Energy Retrofitting
New Additions to Historic Buildings
Accessibility Considerations
Health and Safety Considerations

Although the guidelines were developed to provide assistance in applying the Secretary of the Interior's Standards for Rehabilitation when rehabilitating historic buildings, their approach is simple common sense and can often applied to any structure. The basic concept behind application of the guidelines is to understand what components exist, their value, and then to use treatments that reuse valuable elements.

The following guidelines are primarily those issued by the secretary of the interior in 1976. Portions have been updated to reflect a 1992 edition. A complete, illustrated copy of the guidelines can be obtained from the Government Printing Office in Washington, D.C.

BUILDING EXTERIOR

Masonry

Masonry features (such as brick cornices and door pediments, stone window architraves, terra cotta brackets and railings) as well as masonry surfaces (modelling, tooling, bonding patterns joint size, and color) may be important in defining the historic character of the building. It should be noted that while masonry is among the most durable of historic building materials, it is also the most susceptible to damage by improper maintenance or repair techniques and by harsh or abrasive cleaning methods. Most preservation guidance on masonry thus focuses on such concerns as cleaning and the process of repointing.

Recommended

Identifying, retaining, and preserving masonry features that are important in defining the overall historic character of the building such as walls, brackets, railings, cornices, window architraves, door pediments, steps, and columns, and joint and unit size, tooling and bonding patterns, coatings, and color,

Not Recommended

Removing or radically changing masonry features which are important in defining the overall historic character of the building so that, as a result, the character is diminished.

Replacing or rebuilding a major portion of exterior masonry walls that could be repaired so that, as a result, the building is no longer historic and is essentially new construction.

Applying paint or other coatings such as stucco to masonry that has been historically unpainted or uncoated to create a new appearance.

Removing paint from historically painted masonry.

Radically changing the type of paint or coating or its color.

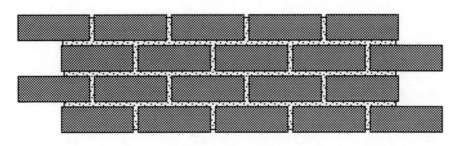

Running Bond

Building Exterior: Masonry (continued)

Recommended	Not Recommended

Recommended

Protecting and maintaining masonry by providing proper drainage so that water does not stand on flat, horizontal surfaces or accumulate in curved decorative features,

Cleaning masonry only when necessary to halt deterioration or remove heavy soiling.

Carrying out masonry surface cleaning tests after it has been determined that such cleaning is necessary. Tests should be observed over a sufficient period of time so that both the immediate effects and the long range effects are known to enable selection of the gentlest method possible.

Cleaning masonry surfaces with the gentlest method possible, such as low pressure water and detergents, using natural bristle brushes.

Inspecting painted masonry surfaces to determine whether repainting is necessary.

Removing damaged or deteriorated paint only to the next sound layer using the gentlest method possible (e. g., hand scraping) prior to repainting.

Applying compatible paint coating systems following proper surface preparation.

Repainting with colors that are historically appropriate to the building and district.

Not Recommended

Failing to evaluate and treat the various causes of mortar joint deterioration such as leaking roofs or gutters, differential settlement of the building, capillary action, or extreme weather exposure.

Cleaning masonry surfaces when they are not heavily soiled to create a new appearance, thus needlessly introducing chemicals or moisture into historic materials.

Cleaning masonry surfaces without testing or without sufficient time for the testing results to be of value.

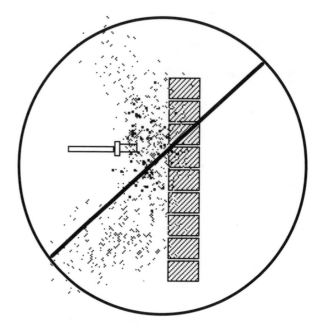

Sandblasting brick or stone surfaces using dry or wet grit or other abrasives. These methods of cleaning permanently erode the surface of the material and accelerate deterioration.

Using a cleaning method that involves water or liquid chemical solutions when there is any possibility of freezing temperature.

Cleaning with chemical products that will damage masonry, such as using acid on limestone or marble, or leaving chemicals on masonry surfaces.

Applying high pressure water cleaning methods that will damage historic masonry and the mortar joints.

Removing paint that is firmly adhering to, and thus protecting, masonry surfaces.

Using methods of removing paint which are destructive to masonry, such as sandblasting, application of caustic solutions, or high pressure waterblasting.

Failing to follow manufacturers' product and application instructions when repainting masonry.

Using new paint colors that are inappropriate to the historic building and district.

Building Exterior: Masonry (continued)

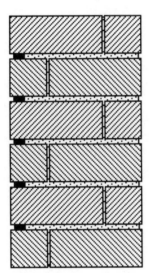

Tuckpointed Brick Wall

In tuckpointing, you remove the old mortar and replace it with new material. The new mortar should extend back at least 1-1/2", or 2-1/2 times the height of the joint.

Recommended	Not Recommended
Evaluating the overall condition of the masonry to determine whether more than protection and maintenance are required, that is, if repairs to the masonry features will be necessary.	Failing to undertake adequate measures to assure the preservation of masonry features.
Repairing masonry walls and other masonry features by repointing the mortar joints where there is evidence of deterioration such as disintegrating mortar, cracks in mortar joints, loose bricks, damp walls, or damaged plasterwork.	Removing nondeteriorated mortar from sound joints, then repointing the entire building to achieve a uniform appearance.
Removing deteriorated mortar by carefully hand-raking the joints to avoid damaging the masonry.	Using electric saws and hammers rather than hand tools to remove deteriorated mortar from joints prior to repointing.
Duplicating old mortar in strength, composition, color, and texture.	Repointing with mortar of high portland cement content (unless it is the content of the historic mortar). This can often create a bond that is stronger than the historic material and can cause damage as a result of the differing coefficient of expansion and the differing porosity of the material and the mortar.
	Repointing with a synthetic caulking compound.
	Using a "scrub" coating technique to repoint instead of traditional repointing methods.
Duplicating old mortar joints in width and in joint profile.	Changing the width or joint profile when repointing.
Repairing stucco by removing the damaged material and patching with new stucco that duplicates the old in strength, composition, color, and texture.	Removing sound stucco; or repairing with new stucco that is stronger than the historic material or does not convey the same visual appearance.
Using mud plaster as a surface coating over unfired, unstabilized adobe because the mud plaster will bond to the adobe.	Applying cement stucco to unfired, unstabilized adobe. Because the cement stucco will not bond properly, moisture can become entrapped between materials, resulting in accelerated deterioration of the adobe.
Cutting damaged concrete back to remove the source of deterioration (often corrosion on metal reinforcement bars). The new patch must be applied carefully so it will bond satisfactorily with, and match, the historic concrete.	Patching concrete without removing the source of deterioration.

Building Exterior: Masonry (continued)

Recommended	Not Recommended
Repairing masonry features by patching, piecing-in, or consolidating the masonry using recognized preservation methods. Repair may also include the limited replacement in kind or with compatible substitute material of those extensively deteriorated or missing parts of masonry features when there are surviving prototypes such as terra cotta brackets or stone balusters.	Replacing an entire masonry feature such as a cornice or balustrade when repair of the masonry and limited replacement of deteriorated or missing parts are appropriate.
	Using a substitute material for the replacement part that does not convey the visual appearance of the surviving parts of the masonry feature or that is physically or chemically incompatible.
Applying new or nonhistoric surface treatments such as water repellent coatings to masonry only after repointing and only if masonry repairs have failed to arrest water penetration problems.	Applying waterproof, water-repellent, or nonhistoric coatings such as stucco to masonry as a substitute for repointing and masonry repairs. Coatings are frequently unnecessary, expensive, and may change the appearance of historic masonry as well as accelerate its deterioration.
Replacing in kind an entire masonry feature that is too deteriorated to repair if the overall form and detailing are still evident using the physical evidence to guide the new work. Examples can include large sections of a wall, a cornice, balustrade, column, or stairway. If using the same kind of material is not technically or economically feasible, then a compatible substitute material may be considered.	Removing a masonry feature that is unrepairable and not replacing it; or replacing it with a new feature that does not convey the same visual appearance.

Design for Missing Historic Features

Recommended	Not Recommended
Designing and installing a new masonry feature such as steps or a door pediment when the historic feature is completely missing. It may be an accurate restoration using historical, pictorial, and physical documentation; or be a new design that is compatible with the size, scale, material, and color of the historic building.	Creating a false historical appearance because the replaced masonry feature is based on insufficient historical, pictorial, and physical documentation.
	Introducing a new masonry feature that is incompatible in size, scale, material, and color.

BUILDING EXTERIOR

Wood

Because it can be easily shaped by sawing, planing, carving, and gouging, wood is the most commonly used material for architectural features, such as clapboards, cornices, brackets, entablatures, shutters, columns and balustrades. These wooden features both functional and decorative may be important in defining the historic character of the building and thus their retention, protection, and repair are of particular importance in rehabilitation projects. (For specific guidance, consult Preservation Brief No. 9 and No. 10 and *Epoxies for Wood Repair in Historic Building*.)

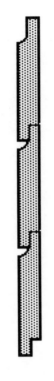

Wood Siding

Recommended

Identifying, retaining, and preserving wood features that are important in defining the overall historic character of the building such as siding, cornices, brackets, window architraves, and doorway pediments, and their paints, finishes, and colors.

Protecting and maintaining wood features by providing proper drainage so that water is not allowed to stand on flat, horizontal surfaces or accumulate in decorative features.

Not Recommended

Removing or radically changing wood features which are important in defining the overall historic character of the building so that, as a result, the character is diminished.

Removing a major portion of the historic wood from a facade instead of repairing or replacing only the deteriorated wood, then reconstructing the facade with new material in order to achieve a uniform or "improved" appearance.

Radically changing the type of finish or its color or accent scheme so that the historic character of the exterior is diminished.

Stripping historically painted surfaces to bare wood, then applying clear finishes or stains in order to create a "natural look."

Stripping paint or varnish to bare wood rather than repairing or reapplying a special finish, i. e., a grained finish to an exterior wood feature such as a front door.

Failing to identify, evaluate, and treat the causes of wood deterioration, including faulty flashing, leaking gutters, cracks and holes in siding, deteriorated caulking in joints and seams, plant material growing too close to wood surfaces, or insect or fungus infestation.

Building Exterior: Wood (continued)

Recommended	Not Recommended
Applying chemical preservatives to wood features such as beam ends or outriggers that are exposed to decay hazards and are traditionally unpainted.	Using chemical preservatives such as creosote which can change the appearance of wood features unless they were used historically.
Retaining coatings such as paint that help protect the wood from moisture and ultraviolet light. Paint removal should be considered only where there is paint surface deterioration and as part of an overall maintenance program which involves repainting or applying other appropriate protective coatings.	Stripping paint or other coatings to reveal bare wood, thus exposing historically coated surfaces to the effects of accelerated weathering.
Inspecting painted wood surfaces to determine whether repainting is necessary or if cleaning is all that is required.	Removing paint that is firmly adhering to, and thus, protecting wood surfaces.
	Replacing an entire wood feature such as a cornice or wall when repair of the wood and limited replacement of deteriorated or missing oarts are appropriate.
	Using substitute material for the replacement part that does not convey the visual appearance of the surviving parts of the wood feature or that is physically or chemically incompatible.
Removing damaged or deteriorated paint to the next sound layer using the gentlest method possible (hand scraping and hand sanding), then repainting.	Using destructive paint removal methods such as a propane or butane torches, sandblasting or waterblasting. These methods can irreversibly damage historic woodwork.
Using with care electric hot-air guns on decorative wood features and electric heat plates on flat wood surfaces when paint is so deteriorated that total removal is necessary prior to repainting.	Using thermal devices improperly so that the historic woodwork is scorched.
Using chemical strippers primarily to supplement other methods such as hand scraping, hand sanding and the above recommended thermal devices. Detachable wooden elements such as shutters, doors, and columns may--with the proper safeguards--be chemically dip-stripped.	Failing to neutralize the wood thoroughly after using chemicals so that new paint does not adhere.
	Allowing detachable wood features to soak too long in a caustic solution so that the wood grain is raised and the surface roughened.

Building Exterior: Wood (continued)

Recommended	Not Recommended
Applying compatible paint coating systems following proper surface preparation.	Failing to follow manufacturers' product and application instructions when repainting exterior woodwork.
Repainting with colors that are appropriate to the historic building and district.	Using new colors that are inappropriate to the historic building or district.
Evaluating the overall condition of the wood to determine whether more than protection and maintenance are required, that is, if repairs to wood features will be necessary.	Failing to undertake adequate measures to assure the preservation of wood features.
Repairing wood features by patching, piecing-in, consolidating, or otherwise reinforcing the wood using recognized preservation methods. Repair may also include the limited replacement in kind or with compatible substitute material of those extensively deteriorated or missing parts of features where there are surviving prototypes such as brackets, moldings, or sections of siding.	Replacing an entire wood feature such as a cornice or wall when repair of the wood and limited replacement of deteriorated or missing parts are appropriate. Using substitute material for the replacement part that does not convey the visual appearance of the surviving parts of the wood feature or that is physically or chemically incompatible.
Replacing in kind an entire wood feature that is too deteriorated to repair--if the overall form and detailing are still evident--using the physical evidence to guide the new work. Examples of wood features include a cornice, entablature or balustrade. If using the same kind of material is not technically or economically feasible, then a compatible substitute material may be considered.	Removing an entire wood feature that is unrepairable and not replacing it; or replacing it with a new feature that does not convey the same visual appearance.

Design for Missing Features

Recommended	Not Recommended
Designing and installing a new wood feature such as a cornice or doorway when the historic feature is completely missing. It may be an accurate restoration using historical, pictorial, and physical documentation; or be a new design that is compatible with the size, scale, material, and color of the historic building.	Creating a false historical appearance because the replaced wood feature is based on insufficient historical, pictorial, and physical documentation. Introducing a new wood feature that is incompatible in size, scale, material, and color.

75

BUILDING EXTERIOR

Architectural Metals

Architectural metal features such as cast-iron facades, porches, and steps; sheet metal cornices, roofs, roof cresting and storefronts, and cast or rolled metal doors, window sash, entablatures, and hardware are often highly decorative and may be important in defining the overall historic character of the building. Their retention, protection, and repair should be a prime consideration in rehabilitation projects. (For specific guidance, consult *Metals in America's Historic Building*.)

Recommended

Identifying, retaining, and preserving architectural metal features such as columns, capitals, window hoods, or stairways that are important in defining the overall historic character of the building, and their finishes and colors. Identification is also critical to differentiate between metals prior to work. Each metal has unique properties and thus requires different treatments.

Protecting and maintaining architectural metals from corrosion by providing proper drainage so that water does not stand on flat, horizontal surfaces or accumulate in curved, decorative features.

Cleaning architectural metals, when necessary, to remove corrosion prior to repainting or applying other appropriate protective coatings.

Not Recommended

Removing or radically changing architectural metal features which are important in defining the overall historic character of the building so that, as a result, the character is diminished.

Removing a major portion of the historic architectural metal from a facade instead of repairing or replacing only the deteriorated metal, then reconstructing the facade with new material in order to create a uniform, or "improved" appearance.

Radically changing the type of finish or its historic color or accent scheme.

Failing to identify, evaluate, and treat the causes of corrosion, such as moisture from leaking roofs or gutters.

Placing incompatible metals together without providing a reliable separation material. Such incompatibility can result in galvanic corrosion of the less noble metal, e. g., copper will corrode cast iron, steel, tin, and aluminum.

Exposing metals which were intended to be protected from the environment.

Applying paint or other coatings to metals such as copper, bronze, or stainless steel that were meant to be exposed.

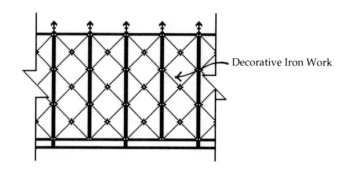

Decorative Iron Work

Art-metal (Fence)

Building Exterior: Architectural Metals (continued)

Recommended	Not Recommended
Identifying the particular type of metal prior to any cleaning procedure and then testing to assure that the gentlest cleaning method possible is selected or determining that cleaning is inappropriate for the particular metal.	Using cleaning methods which alter or damage the historic color, texture, and finish of the metal; or cleaning when it is inappropriate for the metal.
	Removing the patina of historic metal. The patina may be a protective coating on some metals, such as bronze or copper, as well as a significant historc finish.
Cleaning soft metals such as lead, tin, copper, terneplate, and zinc with appropriate chemical methods because their finishes can be easily abraded by blasting methods.	Cleaning soft metals such as lead, tin, copper, terneplate, and zinc with grit blasting which will abrade the surface of the metal.
Using the gentlest methods for cast iron, wrought iron, and steel--hard metals--in order to remove paint buildup and corrosion. If handscraping and wire brushing have proven ineffective, low pressure grit blasting may be used as long as it does not abrade or damage the surface.	Failing to employ gentler methods prior to abrasively cleaning cast iron, wrought iron, steel; or using high pressure grit blasting.
Applying appropriate paint or other coating systems after cleaning in order to decrease the corrosion rate of metals or alloys.	Failing to re-apply protective coating systems to metals or alloys that require them after cleaning so that accelerated corrosion occurs.
Repainting with colors that are appropriate to the historic building or district.	Using colors that are inappropriate to the historic building or district.
Applying an appropriate protective coating such as lacquer to an architectural matal feature such as a bronze door which is subject to heavy pedestrian use.	Failing to assess pedestrian use or new access patterns so that architectural metal features are subject to damage by use or inappropriate maintenance such as salting adjacent sidewalks.
Evaluating the overall condition of the architectural metals to determine whether more than protection and maintenance are required, that is, if repairs to features will be necessary.	Failing to undertake adequate measures to assure the protection of architectural metal features.

Building Exterior: Architectural Metals (continued)

Recommended	Not Recommended
Repairing architectural metal features by patching, splicing, or otherwise reinforcing the metal following recognized preservation methods. Repairs may also include the limited replacement in kind--or with a compatible substitute material--of those extensively deteriorated or missing parts of features when there are surviving prototypes such as porch balusters, column capitals or bases; or porch cresting.	Replacing an entire architectural metal feature such as a column or a balustrade when repair of the metal and limited replacement of deteriorated or missing parts are appropriate.
	Using a substitute material for the replacement part that does not convey the visual appearance of the surviving parts of the architectural metal feature or is physically or chemically incompatible.
Replacing in kind an entire architectural metal feature that is too deteriorated to repair--if the overall form and detaining are still evident--using the physical evidence as a model to reproduce the feature. Examples could include cast iron porch steps or steel sash windows. If using the same kind of material is not technically or economically feasible, then a compatible substitute material may be considered.	Removing an architectural metal feature that is unrepairable and not replacing it; or replacing it with a new architectural metal feature that does not convey the same visual appearance.

Design for Missing Historic Features

Designing and installing a new architectural metal feature such as a metal cornice or cast iron capital when the historic feature is completely missing. It may be an accurate restoration using historical, pictorial, and physical documentation; or be a new design that is compatible with the size, scale, material, and color of the historic building.	Creating a false historical appearance because the replaced architectural metal feature is based on insufficient historical, pictorial, and physical documentation.
	Introducing a new architectural metal feature that is incompatible in size, scale, material, and color.

78

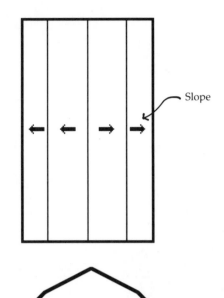

Gambrel Roof

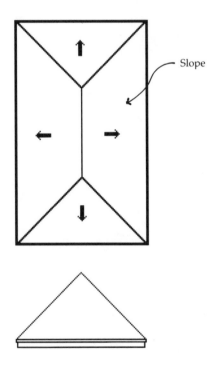

Hip Roof

BUILDING EXTERIOR

Roofs

The roof--with its shape; features such as cresting, dormers, cupolas, and chimneys; and the size, color, and patterning of the roofing materials--can be extremely important in defining the building's overall historic character. In addition to the design role it plays, a weather tight roof is essential to the preservation of the entire structure; thus protecting and rehabilitation project.

Recommended

Identifying, retaining, and preserving roofs--and their functional and decorative features--that are important in defining the overall historic character of the building. This includes the roof's shape, such as hipped, gambrel, and mansard; decorative features such as cupolas, cresting, chimneys, and weather vanes; and roofing material such as slate, wood, clay tile, and metal, as well as its size, color, and patterning.

Protecting and maintaining a roof by cleaning the gutters and downspouts and replacing deteriorated flashing. Roof sheathing should also be checked for proper venting to prevent moisture condensation and water penetration; and to insure that materials are free from insect infestation.

Providing adequate anchorage for roofing material to guard against wind damage and moisture penetration.

Protecting a leaking roof with plywood and building paper until it can be properly repaired.

Not Recommended

Radically changing, damaging, or destroying roofs which are important in defining the overall historic character of the building so that, as a result, the character is diminished.

Removing a major portion of the roof or roofing material that is repairable, then reconstructing it with new material in order to create a uniform, or "improved," appearance.

Changing the configuration of a roof by adding new features such as dormer windows, vents, or skylights so that the historic character is diminished.

Stripping the roof of sound historic material such as slate, clay tile, wood, and architectural metal.

Applying paint or other coatings to roofing material which has been historically uncoated.

Failing to clean and maintain gutters and downspouts properly so that water and debris collect and cause damage to roof fasteners, sheathing, and the underlying structure.

Allowing roof fasteners, such as nails and clips, to corrode so that roofing material is subject to accelerated deterioration.

Permitting a leaking roof to remain unprotected so that accelerated deterioration of historic building materials--masonry, wood, plaster, paint, and structural members--occurs.

Building Exterior: Roofs (continued)

Recommended

Repairing a roof by reinforcing the historic materials which comprise roof features. Repairs will also generally include the limited replacement in kind--or with compatible substitute material--or those extensively deteriorated or missing parts of features when there are surviving prototypes such as cupola louvers, dentils, dormer roofing; or slates, tiles, or wood shingles on a main roof.

Replacing in kind an entire feature of the roof that is too deteriorated to repair--if the overall form and detailing are still evident--using the physical evidence to guide the new work. Examples can include a large section of roofing, or a dormer or chimney. If using the same kind of material is not technically or economically feasible, then a compatible substitute material may be considered.

Design for Missing Historic Features

Designing and constructing a new feature when the historic feature is completely missing, such as a chimney or cupola. It may be an accurate restoration using historical, pictorial, and physical documentation; or be a new design that is compatible with the size, scale, material, and color of the historic building.

Alterations/Additions for the New Use

Installing mechanical and service equipment on the roof such as air conditioning, transformers, or solar collectors when required for the new use so that they are inconspicuous from the public right-of-way and do not damage or obscure character-defining features.

Designing additions to roofs such as residential, office, or storage spaces; elevator housing; decks and terraces; or dormers or skylights when required by the new use so that they are inconspicuous from the public right-of-way and do not damage or obscure character-defining features.

Not Recommended

Replacing an entire roof feature such as a cupola or dormer when repair of the historic materials and limited replacement of deteriorated or missing parts are appropriate.

Failing to reuse intact slate or tile when only the roofing substrate needs replacement.

Using a substitute material for the replacement part that does not convey the visual appearance of the surviving parts of the roof or that is physically or chemically incompatible.

Removing a feature of the roof that is unrepairable, such as a chimney or dormer, and not replacing it; or replacing it with a new feature that does not convey the same visual appearance.

Creating a false historical appearance because the replaced feature is based on insufficient historical, pictorial, and physical documentation.

Introducing a new roof feature that is incompatible in size, scale, material, and color.

Installing mechanical or service equipment so that it damages or obscures character-defining features; or is conspicuous from the public right-of-way.

Radically changing a character-defining roof shape or damaging or destroying character-defining roofing material as a result of incompatible design or improper installation techniques.

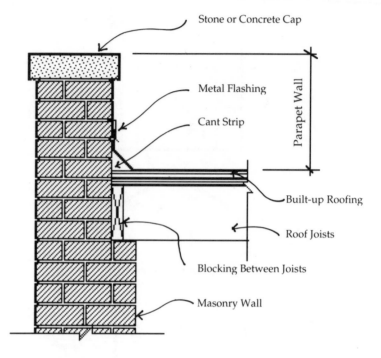

Parapet Wall

(Labels: Stone or Concrete Cap, Metal Flashing, Cant Strip, Built-up Roofing, Roof Joists, Blocking Between Joists, Masonry Wall, Parapet Wall)

BUILDING EXTERIOR

Windows

A highly decorative window with an unusual shape, glazing pattern, or color is most likely identified immediately as a character-defining feature of the building. It is far more difficult, however, to assess the importance of repeated windows on a facade, particularly if they are individually simple in design and material, such as the large, multi-paned sash of many industrial buildings. Because rehabilitation projects frequently include proposals to replace window sash or even entire windows to improve thermal efficiency or to create a new appearance, it is essential that the original windows' contribution to the overall historic character of the building be assessed together with their physical condition before specific repair or replacement work is undertaken.

Recommended

Identifying, retaining, and preserving windows -- and their functional and decorative features -- that are important in defining the overall historic character of the building. Such features can include frames, sash, muntins, glazing, sills, heads, hood molds, panelled or decorated jambs and moldings, and interior and exterior shutters and blinds.

Conducting an in-depth survey of the conditions of existing windows early in rehabilitation planning so that repair and upgrading methods and possible replacement options can be fully explored.

Not Recommended

Removing or radically changing windows which are important in defining the overall historic character of the building so that, as a result, the character is diminished.

Changing the number, location, size, or glazing pattern of windows, through cutting new openings, blocking in windows, and installing replacement sash which does not fit the historic window opening.

Changing the historical appearance of windows through the use of inappropriate designs, materials, finishes, or colors which radically change the sash, depth of reveal, and muntin configuration; the reflectivity and color of the glazing; or the appearance of the frame.

Obscuring historic window trim with metal or other material.

Stripping windows of historic material such as wood, iron, cast iron, and bronze.

Replacing windows solely because of peeling paint, broken glass, stuck sash, and high air infiltration. These conditions, in themselves, are no indication that the windows are beyond repair.

Building Exterior: Windows (continued)

Recommended	Not Recommended
Protecting and maintaining the wood and architectural metal which comprise the window frame, sash, muntins, and surrounds through appropriate surface treatments such as cleaning, rust removal, limited paint removal, and reapplication of protective coating systems.	Failing to provide adequate protection of materials on a cyclical basis so that deterioration of the window results.
Making windows weathertight by recaulking and replacing or installing weatherstripping. These actions also improve thermal efficiency.	Retrofitting or replacing windows rather than maintaining the sash, frame, and glazing.
Evaluating the overall condition of materials to determine whether more than protection and maintenance are required, i.e., if repairs to windows and window features will be required.	Failure to undertake adequate measures to assure the preservation of historic windows.
Repairing window frames and sash by patching, splicing, consolidating, or otherwise reinforcing. Such repair may also include replacement in kind of those parts that are missing when there are surviving prototypes such as architraves, hood molds, sash, sills, and interior or exterior shutters and blinds.	Replacing an entire window when repair of materials and limited replacement of deteriorated or missing parts are appropriate.
	Failing to reuse serviceable window hardware such as brass lifts and sash locks.
	Using a substitute material for the replacement part that does not convey the visual appearance of the surviving parts of the window or that is physically or chemically incompatible.
Replacing in kind an entire window that is too deteriorated to repair--if the overall form and detailing are still evident--using the physical evidence to guide the new work. If using the same kind of material is not technically or economically feasible, then a compatible substitute material may be considered.	Removing a character-defining window that is unrepairable and blocking it in; or replacing it with a new window that does not convey the same visual appearance.

Building Exterior: Windows (continued)

Design for Missing Historic Features

Designing and installing new windows when the historic windows (frame, sash, and glazing) are completely missing. The replacement windows may be an accurate restoration using historical, pictorial, and physical documentation; or be a new design that is compatible with the window openings and the historic character of the building.

Creating a false historical appearance because the replaced window is based on insufficient historical, pictorial, and physical documentation.

Introducing a new design that is incompatible with the historic character of the building.

Alterations/Additions for the New Use

Designing and installing additional windows on rear or other non-character-defining elevations if required by the new use. New window openings may also be cut into exposed party walls. Such design should be compatible with the overall design of the building, but not duplicate the fenestration pattern and detailing of a character-defining elevation.

Installing new windows including frames, sash, and muntin configurations that are incompatible with the building's historic appearance or obscure, damage, or destroy character-defining features.

Providing a setback in the design of dropped ceilings, when they are required for the new use, to allow for the full height of the window openings.

Inserting new floors or furred-down ceilings which cut across the glazed areas of windows so that the exterior form and appearance of the windows are changed.

BUILDING EXTERIOR

Entrances and Porches

Entrances and porches are quite often the focus of historic buildings, particularly when they occur on primary elevations. Together with their functional and decorative features such as doors, steps, balustrades, pilasters, and entablatures, they can be extremely important in defining the overall historic character of a building. Their retention, protection, and repair should always be carefully considered when planning rehabilitation work.

Building Exterior: Entrances and Porches (continued)

Recommended	Not Recommended

Recommended

Identifying, retaining, and preserving entrances--and their functional and decorative features--that are important in defining the overall historic character of the building such as doors, fanlights, sidelights, pilasters, entablatures, columns, balustrades, and stairs.

Protecting and maintaining the masonry, wood, and architectural metal that comprise entrances and porches through appropriate surface treatments such as cleaning, rust removal, limited paint removal, and re-application of protective coating systems.

Evaluating the overall condition of materials to determine whether more than protection and maintenance are required, that is, if repairs to entrance and porch features will be necessary.

Repairing entrances and porches by reinforcing the historic materials. Repair will also generally include the limited replacement in kind--or with compatible substitute material--of those extensively deteriorated or missing parts of repeated features where there are surviving prototypes such as balustrades, cornices, entablatures, columns, sidelights, and stairs.

Replacing in kind an entire entrance or porch that is too deteriorated to repair--if the form and detailing are still evident--using the physical evidence to guide the new work. If using the same kind of material is not technically or economically feasible, then a compatible substitute material may be considered.

Not Recommended

Removing or radically changing entrances and porches which are important in defining the overall historic character of the building so that, as a result, the character is diminished.

Stripping entrances and porches of historic material such as wood, iron, cast iron, terra cotta, tile, and brick.

Removing an entrance or porch because the building has been re-oriented to accommodate a new use.

Cutting new entrances on a primary elevation.

Altering utilitarian or service entrances so they appear to be formal entrances by adding panelled doors, fanlights, and sidelights.

Failing to provide adequate protection to materials on a cyclical basis so that deterioration of entrances and porches results.

Failing to undertake adequate measures to assure the preservation of historic entrances and porches.

Replacing an entire entrance or porch when the repair of materials and limited replacement of parts are appropriate.

Using a substitute material for the replacement parts that does not convey the visual appearance of the surviving parts of the entrance and porch or that is physically or chemically incompatible.

Removing an entrance or porch that is unrepairable and not replacing it; or replacing it with a new entrance or porch that does not convey the same visual appearance.

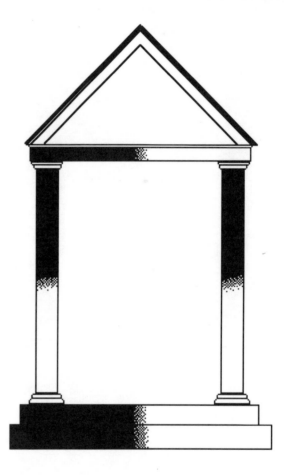

Building Exterior: Entrances and Porches (continued)

Recommended	Not Recommended
Design for Missing Historic Features	
Designing and constructing a new entrance or porch if the historic entrance or porch is completely missing. It may be a restoration based on historical, pictorial, and physical documentation; or be a new design that is compatible with the historic character of the building.	Creating a false historical appearance because the replaced entrance or porch is based on insufficient historical, pictorial, and physical documentation.
	Introducing a new entrance or porch that is incompatible in size, scale, material, and color.
Alterations/Additions for the New Use	
Designing enclosures for historic porches when required by the new use in a manner that preserves the historic character of the building. This can include using large sheets of glass and recessing the enclosure wall behind existing scrollwork, posts, and balustrades.	Enclosing porches in a manner that results in a diminution or loss of historic character such as using solid materials such as wood, stucco, or masonry.
Designing and installing additional entrances or porches when required for the new use in a manner that preserves the historic character of the building, i.e., limiting such alteration to non-character-defining elevations.	Installing secondary service entrances and porches that are incompatible in size and scale with the historic building or obscure, damage, or destroy character-defining features.

BUILDING EXTERIOR

Storefronts

Storefronts are quite often the focus of historic commercial buildings and can thus be extremely important in defining the overall historic character. Because storefronts also play a crucial role in a store's advertising and merchandising strategy to draw customers and increase business, they are often altered to meet the needs of a new business. Particular care is required in planning and accomplishing work on storefronts so that the building's historic character is preserved. (Preservation Brief No. 11 should be consulted.)

Recommended

Identify, retaining, and preserving storefronts--and their functional and decorative features--that are important in defining the overall historic character of the building such as display windows, signs, doors, transoms, kick plates, corner posts, and entablatures.

Protecting and maintaining masonry, wood, and architectural metals which comprise storefronts through appropriate treatments such as cleaning, rust removal, limited paint removal, and reapplication of protective coating systems.

Protecting storefronts against arson and vandalism before work begins by boarding up windows and installing alarm systems that are keyed into local protection on agencies.

Not Recommended

Removing or radically changing storefronts--and their features--which are important in defining the overall historic character of the building so that, as a result, the character is diminished.

Changing the storefront so that it appears residential rather than commercial in character.

Removing historic material from the storefront to create a recessed arcade.

Introducing coach lanterns, mansard overhangings, wood shakes, nonoperable shutters, and small-paned windows if they cannot be documented historically.

Changing the location of a storefront's main entrance.

Failing to provide adequate protection to materials on a cyclical basis so that deterioration of storefront features results.

Permitting entry into the building through unsecured or broken windows and doors so that interior features and finishes are damaged through exposure to weather or through vandalism.

Stripping storefronts of historic material such as wood, cast iron, terra cotta, carrara glass, and brick.

Building Exterior: Storefronts (continued)

Recommended	Not Recommended
Evaluating the overall condition of storefront materials to determine whether more than protection and maintenance are required, that is, if repairs to features will be necessary.	Failing to undertake adequate measures to assure the preservation of the historic storefront.
Repairing storefronts by reinforcing the historic materials. Repairs will also generally include the limited replacement in kind--or with compatible substitute material--of those extensively deteriorated or missing parts of storefronts where there are surviving prototypes such as transoms, kick plates, pilasters, or signs.	Replacing an entire storefront when repair of materials and limited replacement of its parts are appropriate. Using substitute material for the replacement parts that does not convey the same visual appearance as the surviving parts of the storefront or that is physically or chemically incompatible.
Replacing in kind an entire storefront that is too deteriorated to repair--if the overall form and detailing are still evident--using the physical evidence to guide the new work. If using the same material is not technically or economically feasible, then compatible substitute materials may be considered.	Removing a storefront that is unrepairable and not replacing it; or replacing it with a new storefront that does not convey the same visual appearance.

Design for Missing Historic Features.

Recommended	Not Recommended
Designing and constructing a new storefront that is completely missing. It may be an accurate restoration using historical, pictorial, and physical documentation; or be new design that is compatible with the size, scale, material, and color of the historic building. Such new design should generally be flush with the facade; and the treatment of secondary design elements, such as awnings or signs, kept as simple as possible. For example, new signs should fit flush with the existing features of the facade, such as the fascia board or cornice.	Creating a false historical appearance because the replaced storefront is based on insufficient historical, pictorial, and physical documentation. Introducing a new design that is incompatible in size, scale, material, and color. Using new illuminated signs; inappropriately scaled signs and logos; signs that project over the sidewalk unless they were a characteristic feature of the historic building; or other types of signs that obscure, damage, or destroy remaining character-defining features of the historic building.

BUILDING INTERIOR

Structural Systems

If features of the structural system are exposed such as loadbearing brick walls, cast iron columns, roof trusses, posts and beams, vigas, or stone foundation walls, they may be important in defining the building's overall hisyoric character. Unexposed structural features that are not character-defining or an entire structural system may nontheless be significant in the history of building technology; therefore, the structural system should always be examined and evaluated early in the project planning stage to determine both its physical condition and its importance to the building's character or historical significance.

Recommended

Identifying, retaining, and preserving structural systems--and individual features of systems--that are important in defining the overall historic character of the building, such as post and beam systems, trusses, summer beams, vigas, cast iron columns, above-grade stone foundation walls, or loadbearing brick or stone walls.

Protecting and maintaining the structural system by cleaning the roof gutters and downspouts; replacing roof flashing; keeping masonry, wood, and architectural metals in a sound condition; and assuring that structural members are free from insect infestation.

Not Recommended

Removing, covering, or radically changing features of structural systems which are important in defining the overall historic character of the building so that, as a result, the character is diminished.

Putting a new use into the building which could overload the existing structural system; or installing equipment or mechanical systems which could damage the structure.

Demolishing a loadbearing masonry wall that could be augmented and retained, and replacing it with a new wall (i.e., brick or stone), using the historic masonry only as an exterior veneer.

Leaving known structural problems untreated such as deflection of beams, cracking and bowing of walls, or racking of structural members.

Utilizing treatments or products that accelerate the deterioration of structural material such as introducing urea-formaldehyde foam insulation into frame walls.

Failing to provide proper building maintenance so that deterioration of the structural system results. Causes of deterioration include subsurface ground movement, vegetation growing too close to foundation walls, improper grading, fungal rot, and poor interior ventilation that results in condensation.

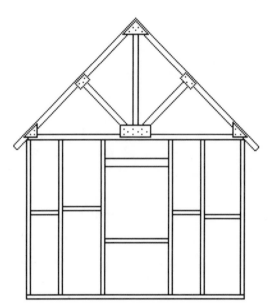

Building Interior: Structural Systems (continued)

Recommended	Not Recommended
Examining and evaluating the physical condition of the structural system and its individual features using nondestructive techniques such as X-ray photography.	Utilizing destructive probing techniques that will damage or destroy structural material.
Repairing the structural system by augmenting or upgrading individual parts or features. For example, weakened structural members such as floor framing can be paired with a new member, braced, or otherwise supplemented and reinforced.	Upgrading the building structurally in a manner that diminishes the historic character of the exterior, such as installing strapping channels or removing a decorative cornice; or that damages interior features or spaces.
	Replacing a structural member or other feature of the structural system when it could be augmented and retained.
Replacing in kind--or with substitute material--those portions or features of the structural system that are either extensively deteriorated or are missing when there are surviving prototypes such as cast iron columns, roof rafters or trusses, or sections of loadbearing walls. Substitute material should convey the same form, design, and overall appearance as the historic feature; and, at a minimum, equal its loadbearing capabilities.	Installing a replacement feature that does not convey the same visual appearance, e.g., replacing an exposed wood summer beam with a steel beam.
	Using substitute material that does not equal the loadbearing capabilities of the historic material and design or is otherwise physically or chemically incompatible.

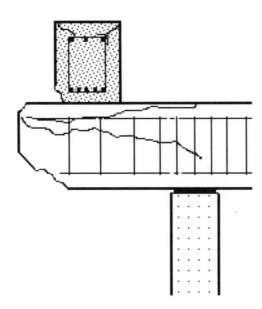

Building Interior: Structural Systems (continued)

Recommended	Not Recommended

Alterations/Additions for New Use

Limiting any new excavations adjacent to historic foundations to avoid undermining the structural stability of the building or adjacent historic buildings. Studies should be done to ascertain potential damage to archeological resources.

Carrying out excavations or regrading adjacent to or within a historic building which could cause the historic foundations to settle, shift, or fail; could have a similar effect on adjacent historic buildings; or could destroy significant archeological resources.

Correcting structural deficiencies in preparation for the new use in a manner that preserves the structural system and individual character-defining features.

Radically changing interior spaces or damaging or destroying features or finishes that are character-defining while trying to correct structural deficiences in preparation for the new use.

Designing and installing new mechanical or electrical systems when required for the new use which minimize the number of cutouts or holes in structural members.

Installing new mechanical and electrical systems or equipment in a manner which results in numerous cuts, splices, or alterations to the structural members.

Adding a new floor when required for the new use if such an alteration does not damage or destroy the structural system or obscure, damage, or destroy character-defining spaces, features, or finishes.

Inserting a new floor when such a radical change damages a structural system or obscures or destroys interior spaces, features, or finishes.

Inserting new floors or furred-down ceilings which cut across the glazed areas of windows so that the exterior form and appearance of the windows are radically changed.

Creating an atrium or a light well to provide natural light when required for the new use in a manner that assures the preservation of the structural system as well as character-defining interior spaces, features, and finishes.

Damaging the structural system or individual features; or radically changing, damaging, or destroying character-defining interior spaces, features, or finishes in order to create an atrium or a light well.

BUILDING INTERIOR

Spaces, Features, and Finishes

An interior floor plan, the arrangement of spaces, and built-in features and applied finishes may be individually or collectively important in defining the historic character of the building. Thus, their identification, retention, protection, and repair should be given prime consideration in every rehabilitation project and caution exercised in pursuing any plan that would radically change character-defining spaces or obscure, damage, or destroy interior features or finishes.

Building Interior: Spaces, Features, and Finishes (continued)

Recommended	Not Recommended

Recommended

Identifying, retaining, and preserving a floor plan or interior spaces that are important in defining the overall historic character of the building. This includes the size, configuration, proportion, and relationship of rooms and corridors; the relationship of features to spaces; and the spaces themselves such as lobbies, reception halls, entrance halls, double parlors, theaters, auditoriums, and important industrial or commercial use spaces.

Not Recommended

Radically changing a floor plan or interior spaces--including individual rooms--which are important in defining the overall historic character of the building so that, as a result, the character is diminished.

Altering the floor plan by demolishing principal walls and partitions to create a new appearance.

Altering or destroying interior spaces by inserting floors, cutting through floors, lowering ceilings, or adding or removing walls.

Relocating an interior feature such as a staircase so that the historic relationship between features and spaces is altered.

Identifying, retaining, and preserving interior features and finishes that are important in defining the overall historic character of the building, including columns, cornices, baseboards, fireplaces and mantels, paneling, light fixtures, hardware, and flooring; and wallpaper, plaster, paint, and finishes such as stenciling, marbling, and graining; and other decorative materials that accent interior features and provide color, texture, and patterning to walls, floors, and ceilings.

Removing or radically changing features and finishes which are important in defining the overall historic character of the building so that, as a result, the character is diminished.

Installing new decorative material that obscures or damages character-defining interior features or finishes.

Removing paint, plaster, or other finishes from historically finished surfaces to create a new appearance (e.g., removing plaster to expose masonry surfaces such as brick walls or a chimney piece).

Applying paint, plaster, or other finishes to surfaces that have been historically unfinished to create a new appearance.

Stripping paint to bare wood rather than repairing or reapplying grained or marbled finishes to features such as doors and paneling.

Radically changing the type of finish or its color, such as painting a previously varnished wood feature.

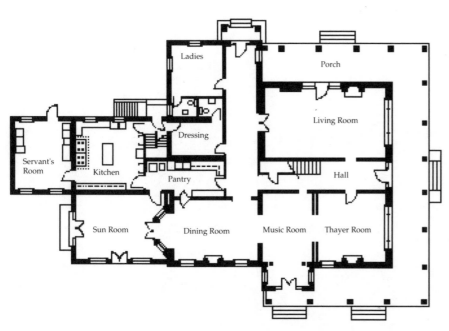

91

Building Interior: Spaces, Features, and Finishes (continued)

Recommended	Not Recommended
Protecting and maintaining masonry, wood, and architectural metals which comprise interior features through appropriate surface treatments such as cleaning, rust removal, limited paint removal, and reapplication of protective coatings systems.	Failing to provide adequate protection to materials on a cyclical basis so that deterioration of interior features results.
Protecting interior features and finishes against arson and vandalism before project work begins, erecting protective fencing, boarding up windows, and installing fire alarm systems that are keyed to local protection agencies.	Permitting entry into historic buildings through unsecured or broken windows and doors so that interior features and finishes are damaged by exposure to weather or through vandalism.
	Stripping interiors of features such as woodwork, doors, windows, light fixtures, copper piping, radiators; or of decorative materials.
Protecting interior features such as a staircase, mantel, or decorative finishes and wall coverings against damage during project work by covering them with heavy canvas or plastic sheets.	Failing to provide proper protection of interior features and finishes during work so that they are gouged, scratched, dented, or otherwise damaged.
Installing protective coverings in areas of heavy pedestrian traffic to protect historic features such as wall coverings, parquet flooring, and paneling.	Failing to take new use patterns into consideration so that interior features and finishes are damaged.
Removing damaged or deteriorated paints and finishes to the next sound layer using the gentlest method possible, then repainting or refinishing using compatible paint or other coating systems.	Using destructive methods such as propane or butane torches or sandblasting to remove paint or other coatings. These methods can irreversibly damage the historic materials that comprise interior features.
Repainting with colors that are appropriate to the historic building.	Using new paint colors that are inappropriate to the historic building.
Limiting abrasive cleaning methods to certain industrial or warehouse buildings where the interior masonry or plaster features do not have distinguishing design, detailing, tooling, or finishes; and where wood features are not finished, molded, beaded, or worked by hand. Abrasive cleaning should only be considered after other, gentler methods have been proven ineffective.	Changing the texture and patina of character-defining features through sandblasting or use of other abrasive methods to remove paint, discoloration or plaster. This includes both exposed wood (including structural members) and masonry.
Evaluating the overall condition of materials to determine whether more than protection and maintenance are required, that is, if repairs to interior features and finishes will be necessary.	Failing to undertake adequate measures to assure the preservation of interior features and finishes.

Building Interior: Spaces, Features, and Finishes (continued)

Recommended	Not Recommended
Repairing interior features and finishes by reinforcing the historic materials. Repair will also generally include the limited replacement in kind--or with compatible substitute material--of those extensively deteriorated or missing parts of repeated features when there are surviving prototypes such as stairs, balustrades, wood panelling, columns, or decorative wall coverings or ornamental tin or plaster ceilings.	Replacing an entire interior feature such as a staircase, paneled wall, parquet floor, or cornice; or finish such as a decorative wall covering or ceiling when repair of materials and limited replacement of such parts are appropriate.
	Using a substitute material for the replacement part that does not convey the visual appearance of the surviving parts or portions of the interior feature or finish or that is physically or chemically incompatible.
Replacing in kind an entire interior feature or finish that is too deteriorated to repair--if the overall form and detailing are still evident--using the physical evidence to guide the new work. Examples could include wainscoting, a tin ceiling, or interior stairs. If using the same kind of material is not technically or economically feasible, then a compatible substitute material may be considered.	Removing a character-defining feature or finish that is unrepairable and not replacing it; or replacing it with a new feature or finish that does not convey the same visual appearance.

Design for Missing Historic Features

Recommended	Not Recommended
Designing and installing a new interior feature or finish if the historic feature or finish is completely missing. This could include missing partitions, stairs, elevators, lighting fixtures, and wall coverings; or even entire rooms if all historic spaces, features, and finishes are missing or have been destroyed by inappropriate "renovations." The design may be a restoration based on historical, pictorial, and physical documentation; or be a new design that is compatible with the historic character of the building, district, or neighborhood.	Creating a false historical appearance because the replaced feature is based on insufficient physical, historical, and pictorial documentation or on information derived from another building.
	Introducing a new interior feature or finish that is incompatible with the scale, design, materials, color, and texture of the surviving interior features and finishes.

Alterations/Additions for the New Use

Recommended	Not Recommended
Accommodating service functions such as bathrooms, mechanical equipment, and office machines required by the building's new use in secondary spaces such as first floor services areas or on upper floors.	Dividing rooms, lowering ceilings, and damaging or obscuring character-defining features such as fireplaces, niches, stairways or alcoves, so that a new use can be accommodated in the building.
Reusing decorative material or features that have had to be removed during the rehabilitation work including wall and baseboard trim, door molding, panelled doors, and simple wainscoting; and relocating such material of features in areas appropriate to their historic placement.	Discarding historic material when it can be reused within the rehabilitation project or relocating it in historically inappropriate areas.

Building Interior: Spaces, Features, and Finishes (continued)

Recommended	Not Recommended
Installing permanent partitions in secondary spaces; removable partitions that do not destroy the sense of space should be installed when the new use requires the subdivision of character-defining interior spaces.	Installing permanent partitions that damage or obscure character-defining spaces, features, or finishes.
Enclosing an interior stairway where required by code, so that its character is retained. In many cases, glazed fire rated walls may be used.	Enclosing an interior stairway with fire rated construction so that the stairwell space or any character-defining features are destroyed.
Placing new code-required stairways or elevators in secondary and service areas of the historic building.	Radically changing, damaging, or destroying, character-defining interior spaces, features, or finishes; or damaging the structural system in order to create an atrium or light well.
Creating an atrium or a light well to provide natural light when required for the new use in a manner that preserves character-defining interior spaces, features, and finishes as well as the structural system.	Destroying character-defining interior spaces, features, or finishes; or damaging the structural system in order to create an atrium or light well.
Adding a new floor if required for the new use in a manner that preserves character-defining structural features, and interior spaces, features, and finishes.	Inserting a new floor within a building that alters or destroys the fenestration; radically changes a character-defining interior space; or obscures, damages, or destroys decorative detailing.

BUILDING INTERIOR

Mechanical Systems

The visible features of historic heating, lighting, air conditioning and plumbing systems may sometimes help define the overall historic character of the building and should thus be retained and repaired, whenever possible. The systems themselves (the compressors, boilers, generators and their ductwork, wiring, and pipes) will generally either need to be upgraded, augmented, or entirely replaced in order to accommodate the new use and to meet code requirements. Less frequently, individual portions of a system or an entire system are significant in the history of building technology, therefore, the identification of character-defining features or historically significant systems should take place together with an evaluation of their physical condition early in project planning.

Recommended	Not Recommended
Identifying, retaining, and preserving visible features of early mechanical systems that are important in defining the overall historic character of the building, such as radiators, vents, fans, grilles, plumbing fixtures, switch plates, and lights.	Removing or radically changing features of mechanical systems that are important in defining the overall historic character of the building so that, as a result, the character is diminished.
Protecting and maintaining mechanical, plumbing, and electrical systems and their features through cyclical cleaning and other appropriate measures.	Failing to provide adequate protection of materials on a cyclical basis so that deterioration of mechanical systems and their visible features results.
Preventing accelerated deterioration of mechanical systems by providing adequate ventilation of attics, crawlspaces, and cellars so that moisture problems are avoided.	Enclosing mechanical systems in areas that are not adequately ventilated so that deterioration of the systems results.
Improving the energy efficiency of existing mechanical system to help reduce the need for elaborate new equipment. Consideration should be given to installing storm windows, insulating attic crawlspace, or adding awnings, if appropriate.	Installing unnecessary air conditioning or climate control systems which can add excessive moisture to the building. This additional moisture can either condense inside, damaging interior surfaces, or adjacent materials as it migrates.
Repairing mechanical systems by augmenting or upgrading system parts, such as installing new pipes and ducts; rewiring; or adding new compressors or boilers.	Replacing a mechanical system or its functional parts when it could be upgraded and retained.

Building Interior: Mechanical Systems (continued)

Recommended	Not Recommended
Replacing in kind--or with compatible substitute material--those visible features of mechanical systems that are either extensively deteriorated or are missing when there are surviving prototypes such as ceiling fans, switch plates, radiators, grilles, or plumbing fixtures.	Installing a replacement feature that does not convey the same visual appearance.

Alterations/Additions for the New Use

Recommended	Not Recommended
Installing a completely new mechanical system if required for the new use so that it causes the least alteration possible to the building's floor plan, the exterior elevations, and the least damage to historic building material.	Installing a new mechanical system so that character-defining structural or interior features are radically changed, damaged, or destroyed.
Providing adequate structural support for new mechanical equipment.	Failing to consider the weight and design of new mechanical equipment so that, as a result, historic structural members or finished surfaces are weakened or cracked.
Installing the vertical runs of ducts, pipes, and cables in closets, service rooms, and wall cavities.	Installing vertical runs of ducts, pipes, and cables in places where they will obscure character-defining features.
	Concealing mechanical equipment in walls or ceilings in a manner that requires the removal of historic building material.
	Installing "dropped" acoustical ceilings to hide mechanical equipment when this destroys the proportions of character-defining interior spaces.
Installing air conditioning units if required by the new use in such a manner that the historic materials and features are not damaged or obscured.	Cutting through features such as masonry walls in order to install air conditioning units.
Installing heating/air conditioning units in the window frames in such a manner that the sash and frames are protected. Window installations should be considered only when viable heating/cooling systems would result in significant damage to historic materials.	Radically changing the appearance of the historic building or damaging or destroying windows by installing heating/air conditioning units in historic window frames.

BUILDING SITE

The relationship between a historic building or buildings and landscape features within a property's boundaries-- or the building site--helps to define the historic character and should be considered an integral part of overall planning for rehabilitation project work.

Recommended	Not Recommended
Identifying, retaining, and preserving buildings and their features as well as features of the site that are important in defining its overall historic character. Site features can include driveways, walkways, lighting, fencing, signs, benches, fountains, wells, terraces, canal systems, plants and trees, berms, and drainage or irrigation ditches; and archeological features that are important in defining the history of the site.	Removing or radically changing buildings and their features or site features which are important in defining the overall historic character of the building site so that, as a result, the character is diminished.
Retaining the historic relationship between buildings, landscape features, and open space.	Removing or relocating historic buildings or landscape features, thus destroying the historic relationship between buildings, landscape features, and open space.
	Removing or relocating historic buildings on a site or in a complex of related historic structures--such as a mill complex or farm--thus diminishing the historic character of the site or complex.
	Moving buildings onto the site, thus creating a false historical appearance.
	Radically changing the grade level of the site. For example, changing the grade adjacent to a building to permit development of a formerly below-grade area that would drastically change the historic relationship of the building to its site.
Protecting and maintaining buildings and the site by providing proper drainage to assure that water does not erode foundation walls; drain toward the building; or erode the historic landscape.	Failing to maintain site drainage so that buildings and site features are damaged or destroyed; or, alternatively, changing the site grading so that water no longer drains properly.
Minimizing disturbance of terrain around buildings or elsewhere on the site, thus reducing the possibility of destroying unknown archeological materials.	Introducing heavy machinery or equipment into areas where their presence may disturb archeological materials.

Building Site (continued)

Recommended	Not Recommended
Surveying and documentating areas where major terrain alteration is likely to impact important archeological sites.	Failing to survey the building site prior to the beginning of rehabilitation work which results in damage to, or destruction of, important landscape features or archeological resources.
Protecting, e.g., preserving in place known archeological resources.	Leaving known archeological material unprotected so that it is damaged during rehabilitation work.
Planning and carrying out any necessary investigation using professional archeologists and modern archeological methods when preservation in place is not feasible.	Permitting unqualified project personnel to perform data recovery so that improper methodology results in the loss of important archeological material.
Preserving important landscape features, including ongoing maintenance of historic plant material.	Allowing important landscape features to be lost or damaged due to a lack of maintenance.
Protecting the building and other features of the site against arson and vandalism before rehabilitation work begins, i.e., erecting protective fencing and installing alarm systems that are keyed into local protection agencies.	Permitting buildings and site features to remain unprotected so that plant materials, fencing, walkways, archeological features, etc., are damaged or destroyed.
	Removing or destroying features from the building or site such as wood siding, iron fencing, masonry balustrades, or plant material.
Providing continued protection of masonry, wood, and architectural metals which comprise building and site features through appropriate surface treatments such as cleaning, rust removal, limited paint removal, and reapplication of protective coating systems; and continued protection and maintenance of landscape features, including plant material.	Failing to provide adequate protection of materials on a cyclical basis so that deterioration of building and site features results.
Evaluating the overall condition of materials to determine whether more than protection and maintenance are required, that is, if repairs to building and site features will be necessary.	Failing to undertake adequate measures to assure the preservation of building and site features.
Repairing features of buildings and the site by reinforcing the historic materials.	Replacing an entire feature of the building or site such as a fence, walkway, or driveway when repair of materials and limited replacement of deteriorated or missing parts are appropriate.
	Using a substitute material for the replacement part that does not convey the visual appearance of the surviving parts of the building or site feature or that is physically or chemically incompatible.

Building Site (continued)

Recommended	Not Recommended
Replacing in kind an entire feature of the building or site that is too deteriorated to repair if the overall form and detailing are still evident.	Removing a feature of the building or site that is unrepairable and not replacing it; or replacing it with a new feature that does not convey the same visual appearance.
Replacing deteriorated or damaged landscape features in kind.	Adding conjectural landscape features to the site such as period reproduction lamps, fences, fountains, or vegetation that is historically inappropriate, thus creating a false sense of historic development.

Design for Missing Historic Features

Designing and constructing a new feature of a building or site when the historic feature is completely missing, such as an outbuilding, terrace, or driveway. It may be based on historical, pictorial, and physical documentation; or be a new design that is compatible with the historic character of the building and site.	Creating a false historical appearance because the replaced feature is based on insufficient historical, pictorial, and physical documentation.
	Introducing a new building or site feature that is out of scale or otherwise inappropriate.
	Introducing a new landscape feature or plant material that is visually incompatible with the site or that destroys site patterns or vistas.

Alterations/Additions for the New Use

Designing new onsite parking, loading docks, or ramps when required by the new use so that they are as unobtrusive as possible and assure the preservation of character-defining features of the site.	Locating any new construction on the building where important landscape features will be damaged or destroyed, for example removing a lawn and walkway and installing a parking lot.
Designing new exterior additions to historic buildings or adjacent new construction which are compatible with the historic character of the site and which preserve the historic relationship between a building or building's landscape features and open space.	Placing parking facilities directly adjacent to historic buildings where automobiles may cause damage to the buildings' or landscape features or be intrusive to the building site.
	Introducing new construction onto the building site which is visually incompatible in terms of size, scale, design, materials, color, and texture or which destroys historic relationships on the site.
Removing nonsignificant buildings, additions, or site features which detract from the historic character of the site.	Removing a historic building in a complex, a building feature, or a site feature which is important in defining the historic character of the site.

SETTING

District or Neighborhood

The relationship between historic buildings, and streetscape and landscape features within a historic district or neighborhood helps to define the historic character and therefore should always be a part of the rehabilitation plans.

Recommended	Not Recommended
Identifying, retaining, and preserving buildings and streetscape, and landscape features which are important in defining the overall historic character of the district or neighborhood. Such features can include streets, alleys, paving, walkways, street lights, signs, benches, parks and gardens, and trees.	Removing or radically changing those features of the district or neighborhood which are important in defining the historic character.
Retaining the historic relationship between buildings, and streetscape and landscape features such as a town square comprised of row houses and stores surrounding a communal park or open space.	Destroying streetscape and landscape features by widening existing streets, changing paving material, or introducing inappropriately located new streets or parking lots.
	Removing or relocating historic buildings, or features of the streetscape and landscape, thus destroying the historic relationship within the setting.
Protecting and maintaining the historic masonry, wood, and architectural metals which comprise building and streetscape features, through appropriate surface treatments such as cleaning, rust removal, limited paint removal, and reapplication of protective coating systems; and protecting and maintaining landscape features, including plant material.	Failing to provide adequate protection of materials on a cyclical basis so that deterioration of building, streetscape, and landscape features results.
Protecting buildings, paving, iron fencing, etc., against arson and vandalism before rehabilitation work begins by erecting protective fencing and installing alarm systems that are keyed into local protection on agencies.	Permitting buildings to remain unprotected so that windows are broken and interior features are damaged.
	Stripping features from buildings or the streetscape such as wood siding, iron fencing, or terra-cotta balusters; or removing or destroying landscape features, including plant material.

Setting: District or Neighborhood (continued)

Recommended	Not Recommended
Evaluating the overall condition of materials to determine whether more than protection and maintenance are required, that is, if repairs to building and site features will be necessary.	Failing to undertake adequate measures to assure the preservation of building and site features.
Repairing features of buildings and the site by reinforcing the historic materials.	Replacing an entire feature of the building or site such as a fence, walkway, or driveway when repair of materials and limited replacement of deteriorated or missing parts are appropriate.
	Using a substitute material for the replacement part that does not convey the visual appearance of the surviving parts of the building or site feature or that is physically, chemically, or ecologically incompatible.
Replacing in kind an entire feature of the building or site that is too deteriorated to repair--if the overall form and detailing are still evident--using the physical evidence to guide the new work. This could include an entrance or porch, walkway, or fountain. If using the same kind of material is not technically or economically feasible, then a compatible substitute material may be considered.	Removing a feature of the building or site that is unrepairable and not replacing it; or replacing it with a new feature that does not convey the same visual appearance.

Design for Missing Historic Features

Designing and constructing a new feature of a building or site when the historic feature is completely missing, such as an outbuilding, terrace, or driveway. It may be based on historical, pictorial, and physical documentation; or be a new design that is compatible with the historic character of the building and site.	Creating a false historical appearance because the replaced feature is based on insufficient historical, pictorial, and physical documentation.
	Introducing a new building or site feature that is out of scale or otherwise inappropriate.

Alterations/Additions for the New Use

Designing new onsite parking, loading docks, or ramps when required by the new use so that they are as unobtrusive as possible and assure the preservation of character-defining features of the site.	Placing parking facilities directly adjacent to historic buildings which cause damage to historic landscape features, including removal of plant material, relocation of paths and walkways, or blocking of alleys.
Designing new exterior additions to historic buildings or adjacent new construction which is compatible with the historic character of the site and which preserve the historic relationship between a building or building's landscape features, and open space.	Introducing new construction into historic districts that which is visually incompatible or that destroys historic relationships withinthe setting.

Setting: District or Neighborhood (continued)

Recommended

Removing nonsignificant building's additions, or site features which detract from the historic character of the site.

ENERGY CONSERVATION

Some character-defining features of a building or site such as cupolas, shutters, transoms, skylights, sun rooms, porches, and plantings also play a secondary, energy conserving role. Therefore, prior to retrofitting historic buildings to make them more energy efficient, the first step should always be to identify and evaluate the existing historic features to assess their inherent energy-conserving potential. If it is determined that retrofitting measures are necessary, then such work needs to be carried out with particular care to ensure that the building's historic character is preserved in the process of rehabilitation.

Recommended

District/Neighborhood

Maintain those existing landscape features which moderate the effects of the climate on the setting such as deciduous trees, evergreen windblocks, and lakes or ponds.

Building Site

Retaining plant materials, trees, and landscape features, especially those which perform passive solar energy functions such as sun shading and wind breaks.

Installing freestanding solar collectors in a manner that preserves the historic property's character-defining features.

Designing attached solar collectors, including solar greenhouses, so that the character-defining features of the property are preserved.

Not Recommended

Removing a historic building, building feature, or landscape feature that is important in defining the historic character of the setting.

Not Recommended

Stripping the setting of landscape features and landforms so that the effects of the wind, rain, and sun result in accelerated deterioration of historic materials.

Removing plant materials, trees, and landscape features, so that they no longer perform passive solar energy functions.

Installing freestanding solar collectors that obscure, damage, or destroy historic landscape or archaeological features.

Locating solar collectors where they radically change the property's appearance; or damage or destroy character-defining features.

Energy Conservation (continued)

Recommended	Not Recommended
Masonry/Wood/Architectural Metals	
Installing thermal insulation in attics and in unheated cellars and crawlspaces to increase the efficiency of the existing mechanical systems.	Applying thermal insulation with a high moisture content into wall cavities in an attempt to reduce energy consumption.
Installing insultating material on the inside of masonry walls to increase energy efficiency where there is no character-defining interior molding around the window or other interior architectural detailing.	Resurfacing historic building materials with more energy efficient but incompatible materials, such as covering historic masonry with exterior insulation.
Installing passive solar devices such as a glazed "trombe" wall on a rear or inconspicuous side of the historic building.	Installing passive solar devices such as an attached glazed "trombe" wall on primary or other highly visible elevations; or where historic material must be removed or obscured.
Roofs	
Placing solar collectors on non character- defining roofs or roofs of nonhistoric adjacent buildings.	Placing solar collectors on roofs when such collectors change the historic roof line or obscure the relationship of the roof to character-defining roof features such as dormers, skylights, and chimneys.
Windows	
Utilizing the inherent energy conserving features of a building by maintaining windows and louvered blinds in good operable condition for natural ventilation.	Removing historic shading devices rather than keeping the m in an operable condition.
Improving thermal efficiency with weatherstripping, storm windows, caulking, interior shades, and, if historically appropriate, blinds and awnings.	Replacing historic multi-pane sash with new thermal sash utilizing false muntins.
Installing interior storm windows with air-tight gaskets, ventilating holes, and/or removable clips to insure proper maintenance and to avoid condensation damage to historic windows.	Installing interior storm windows that allow moisture to accumulate and damage the window.
Installing exterior storm windows which do not damage or obscure the windows and frames'	Installing new exterior storm windows which are inappropriate in size or color, which are inoperable.
	Replacing windows or transoms with fixed thermal glazing or permitting windows and transoms to remain inoperable rather than utilizing them for their energy conserving potential.

Energy Conservation (continued)

Recommended	Not Recommended

Windows

Considering the use of lightly tinted glazing on non-character-defining elevations if other energy retrofitting alternatives are not possible.

Using tinted or reflective glazing on character-defining or other conspicuous elevations.

Entrances and Porches

Utilizing the inherent energy conserving features of a building by maintaining porches, and double vestibule entrances, in good condition so that they can retain heat or block the sun and provide natural ventilation.

Enclosing porches located on character-defining elevations to create passive solar collectors or airlock vestibules. Such enclosures can destroy the historic appearance of the building.

Interior Features

Retaining historic interior shutters and transoms for their inherent energy conserving features.

Removing historic interior features which play a secondary energy conserving role.

New Additions to Historic Buildings

Placing new additions that have an energy conserving function such as a solar greenhouse on non-character-defining elevations.

Installing new additions such as multistory solar greenhouse additions which obscure, damage, destroy character-defining features.

Mechanical Systems

Installing thermal insulation in attics and in unheated cellars and crawlspace to conserve energy.

Replacing existing mechanical systems that could be repaired for continued use.

NEW ADDITIONS TO HISTORIC BUILDINGS

An attached exterior addition to a historic building expands its "outer limits" to create a new profile. Because such expansion has the capability to radically change the historic appearance, an exterior addition should be considered only after it has been determined that the new use cannot be successfully met by altering non-character-defining interior spaces. If the new use cannot be met in this way, then an attached exterior addition is usually an acceptable alternative. New additions should be designed and constructed so that the character-defining features of the historic building are not radically changed, obscured, damaged, or destroyed in the process of rehabilitation. New design should always be clearly differentiated so that the addition does not appear to be part of the historic resources.

Recommended

Placing functions and services required for the new use in non-character-defining interior spaces rather than installing a new addition.

Constructing a new addition so that there is the least possible loss of historic materials and so that character-defining features are not obscured, damaged, or destroyed.

Locating the attached exterior addition at the rear or on an inconspicuous side of a historic building; and limiting its size and scale in relationship to the historic building.

Designing new additions in a manner that makes clear what is historic and what's new.

Not Recommended

Expanding the size of the historic building by constructing a new addition when the new use could be met by altering non-character-defining interior spaces.

Attaching a new addition so that the character-defining features of the historic building are obscured, damaged, or destroyed.

Designing a new addition so that its size and scale in relation to the historic building are out of proportion, thus diminishing the historic character.

Duplicating the exact form, material, style, and detailing of the historic building in the new addition so that the new work appears to be part of the historic building.

Imitating a historic style or period of architecture in new additions, especially for contemporary uses such as drive-in banks or garages.

New Additions To Historic Buildings (continued)

Recommended

Considering the attached exterior addition both in terms of the new use and the appearance of other buildings in the historic district or neighborhood. Design for the new work may be contemporary or may reference design motifs from the historic building. In either case, it should always be clearly differentiated from the historic building and be compatible in terms of mass, materials, relationship of solids to voids, and color.

Placing new additions such as balconies and greenhouses on non-character-defining elevations and limiting the size and scale in relationship to the historic building.

Designing additional stories, when required for the new use, that are set back from the wall plane and are as inconspicuous as possible when viewed from the street.

Not Recommended

Designing and constructing new additions that result in the diminution or loss of the historic character of the resource, including its design, materials, workmanship, location, or setting.

Using the same wall plane, roof line, cornice height, materials, siding lap, or window type to make additions appear to be a part of the historic building.

Designing new additions such as multistory greenhouse additions that obscure, damage, or destroy character-defining features of the historic building.

Constructing additional stories so that the historic appearance of the building is radically changed.

ACCESSIBILITY CONSIDERATIONS

It is often necessary to make modifications to a historic property so that it can comply with current accessibility code requirements. Accessibility to certain historic buildings and sites is required by law. Providing access must be carefully planned and undertaken so that it does not result in a loss of character-defining spaces, features, and fininhes. The goal is to provide the highest level of access with the lowest level of impact.

Recommended

Identifying the building's character-defining spaces, features, and finishes so that accessibility code-required work will not result in their damage or loss.

Complying with barrier-free access requirements in such a manner that character-defining spaces, features, and finishes are preserved.

Not Recommended

Undertaking code-required alterations before identifying those spaces, features or finishes which are character-defining and must therefore be preserved.

Altering, damaging, or destroying character-defining features in attempting to comply with accessibility requirements.

Accessibility Considerations (continued)

Recommended	Not Recommended
Working with local disability groups, access specialists, and historic preservation specialist to determine the most appropriate solution to access problems.	Making changes to buildings without first seeking expert advice from access specialists and historic preservationists, to determine solutions.
Providing barrier-free access that promotes independence for the disabled person to the highest degree practicable, while preserving significant historic features.	Providing access modifications that do not provide a reasonable balance between independent, safe access and preservation of historic features.
designing new or additional means of access that are compatible with the historic property and its setting.	Designing new or additional means of access without considering the impact on the historic property and its setting.

HEALTH AND SAFETY CONSIDERATIONS

As a part of the new use, it is often necessary to make modifications to a historic building so that it can comply with current health, safety, and code requirements. Such work needs to be carefully planned and undertaken so that it does not result in a loss of character-defining spaces, features, and finishes.

Recommended	Not Recommended
Identifying the historic building's character-defining spaces, features, and finishes so that code-required work will not result in their damage or Loss.	Undertaking code-required alterations to a building or site before identifying those spaces, features, or finishes which are character-defining and must therefore be preserved.
Complying with health and safety codes, including seismic codes and barrier-free access requirements, in such a manner that character-defining spaces, features, and finishes are preserved.	Altering, damaging, or destroying character-defining spaces, features, and finishes while making modifications to a building or site to comply with safety codes.
Removing toxic building materials only after thorough testing has been conducted and only after less invasive abatement methods have been shown to be inadequate.	Destroying historic interior features and finishes without careful testing and without considering less invasive abatement methods
Providing workers with appropriate personal protective equipment for hazards found in the worksite.	Removing unhealthful building materials without regard to personal and environmental safety.
Working with local code officials to investigate alternative life safety measures or variances available under some codes so that alterations and additions to historic buildings can be avoided.	Making changes to historic buildings without first seeking alternatives to code requirements.

Health and Safety Considerations (continued)

Recommended	Not Recommended
Upgrading historic stairways and elevators to meet health and safety codes in a manner that assures their preservation, i. e., so that they are not damaged or obscured.	Damaging or obscuring historic stairways and elevators or altering adjacent spaces in the process of doing work to meet code requirements.
Installing sensitively designed fire suppression systems, such as a sprinkler system for wood frame mill buildings, instead of applying fire-resistant sheathing to character-defining features.	Covering character-defining wood features with fire-resistant sheathing which results in altering their visual appearance.
Applying fire-retardant coating, such as intumescent paints, which expand during fire to add thermal protection to steel.	Using fire-retardant coatings if they damage or obscure character-defining features.
Adding a new stairway or elevator to meet health and safety codes in a manner that preserves adjacent character-defining features and spaces.	Radically changing, damaging, or destroying character-defining spaces, features, or finishes when adding a new code-required stairway or elevator.
Placing a code-required stairway or elevator that cannot be accommodated within the historic building in a new exterior addition. Such an addition should be located at the rear of the building or on an inconspicuous side; and its size and scale limited in relationship to the historic building.	Constructing a new addition to accommodate code-required stairs and elevators on character-defining elevations highly visible from the street; or where it obscures, damages or destroys character-defining features.

The words, symbols, and icons listed in this illustrated glossary are commonly used as notations on working drawings or in construction specifications, but may defy simple definition. At times their definitions will differ from those used by the general public. In other cases, the terms are not normally used in everyday conversations outside of the design and construction industry. There are also numerous terms used on plans and in specifications that are not found in this chapter. Their definitions are either commonly known or easily deciphered.

admixture

A material added to a concrete mix, other than water, aggregate, and cement. An admixture may accelerate the setting time of concrete, or add color, or increase strength.

adobe

Unfired brick dried in the sun. Adobe construction is used extensively in the southwestern part of the United States.

aerated concrete

This is a term found on plans and in specifications. It refers to a lightweight concrete that is used for toppings or subfloors and applied in relatively thin layers.

aggregate

As it is used on plans and in specifications, aggregate refers to the coarse stone or gravel that is used in concrete mixes. This material can be made up of any type of stone of a variety of sizes. After the concrete is set, the aggregate is generally not visible. However, the construction documents can call for the final concrete finish to have "exposed aggregate." This can be accomplished in a number of ways, such as by sandblasting or bush-hammering the concrete surface after it has cured, or by washing the finished surface before the concrete has fully set.

AIA

Abbreviation for the American Institute of Architects, 1735 New York Avenue, NW, Washington, DC 20006. When following the name of an architect, this abbreviation indicates that the architect is a corporate member of the institute. An individual can be an architect without being a member of the AIA, but cannot use the letters AIA without being an architect.

air duct

A pipe or tube, round, square or rectangular, for conducting air in a ventilation system.

air-entrained concrete

Concrete containing an agent that traps minute bubbles of air within the concrete, making it more resistant to freeze-thaw cycles. In specifications, air-entrained concrete is designated by the letter "A," such as "Type IA," or "Type IIA."

alteration

A term used in building codes that generally refers to changes to a structure that do not increase or decrease any of its exterior dimensions, or to any changes to the structural members of the building.

angle

On plans and in specifications, the reference to an angle could refer to either the inclination of one straight line to another, the space between two straight lines, or a structural member, generally made of metal, used to support some element of a structure. When referring to a metal angle, the terms "angle iron" or "angle cleat" may be used.

anodizing

A method of coating aluminum with a film of aluminum oxide through an electric process in a chrome-acid solution. The film can be clear or tones of bronze or black.

apse

The projecting portion of a building, usually semicircular in plan.

arch

A term used to describe a curved, pointed, or flat structural member supported at its sides or ends and used to span an opening.

architect

An individual licensed (registered) to design and oversee the construction of buildings. Each state within the United States and most foreign countries provide for the testing and licensing of architects.

Architectural Graphic Standards

A publication of the standards used in architectural practice. Also referred to as Ramsey-Sleeper.

architrave cornice

An entablature of an architrave and cornice, without a frieze.

area

When used on plans, the word "area" can refer to a function, such as living area, or it can refer to the square footage of a space, such as 120 sf in area.

areaway

An open space around a subsurface window or door. It is most often used to provide light and ventilation to basement or cellar spaces.

art metal

Metal that has been shaped or stamped into art forms, such as pressed-tin ceilings, detailed metal cornices, and iron fences.

asbestos

A type of mineral fiber that was formerly used extensively for insulation around ducts and pipes as heat shields and in building materials, such as exterior wall and roof shingles. (Recent findings have determined that airborne asbestos fibers pose serious health risks and should be removed from all buildings.)

ashlar

As generally used, ashlar refers to sawed, dressed, tooled, or quarry-faced stone.

ASTM

The letters ASTM stand for the American Society for Testing and Materials. This reference will be found most often in specifications where a material or (building) system must meet a minimum standard of quality or operation. The letters ASTM will generally be followed by a series of numbers and characters representing the specific standard.

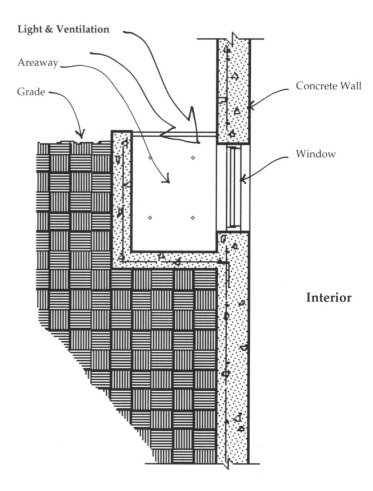

Light & Ventilation

Areaway

Grade

Concrete Wall

Window

Interior

Areaway

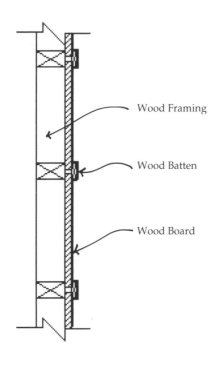

Board & Batten Construction

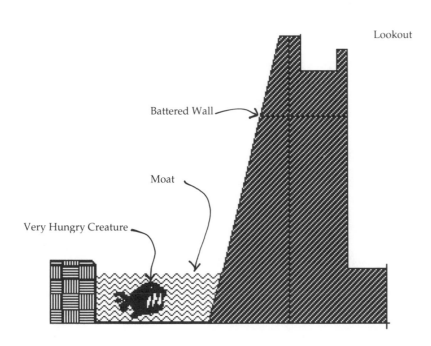

Battered Wall (as used in the Middle Ages)

atrium

A large open hallway or lobby with galleries at each floor level on three or more sides.

backfill

Dirt or other material used to build up the ground around foundation walls.

backing brick

Brick used on the inner part of a brick wall, usually of lesser quality than a face brick.

balloon framing

A method of construction in which wall studs extend in one piece from the first floor of a building up to the roof plate.

baluster

An upright support for a stair or balcony railing.

bar spacing

When used on plans, this refers to the spacing of reinforcing bars in concrete construction. Bar spacing is measured from the center of one bar to the center of the adjacent one.

For example: reinforcing bars, 3/8" round spaced 12" on center in each direction--vertically and horizontally.

batten

A batten is generally used on the exterior of buildings in wood frame construction. It is a wood strip that covers the vertical joint of siding in "board and batten" construction.

batter

Not a pancake mix -- when used as an architectural term, batter refers to a receding upward slope of a wall. In past times this would have been found in fortress construction. First you would have to cross a moat, and then scale a battered wall. In contemporary construction it is a design element.

batter board

In laying out a construction site -- a batter board is used to help establish the corners of an excavation. Nails would be placed in the board to hold a stretched cord marking the outline of the building.

batt insulation

Typically, a presized blanket of mineral-fiber insulation placed between wall, floor, ceiling, or roof framing members.

bay window

A window, of any shape, projecting out from a building and forming a recess in the building interior.

bead

Generally found in detailed work, a bead is a round or semicircular molding.

beam

A structural framing member used to support loads over an opening. Beams can be made up of many different materials--steel, wood, timber, concrete, or a combination of materials.

belt course

A molded or specially sized course of stone or brick carried at the same level around a building.

bent bar

This reference will generally be found on structural plans. It refers to reinforcing bars that are bent to a prescribed shape.

bevel siding

A type of wood siding which has one edge thicker than the other.

bib valve

In plumbing, a common valve used to open and close a water valve.

bifolds

Doors, generally light in weight and used on closets.

blanket insulation

A lightweight fiber insulation, such as fiberglass, supplied in rolls.

bleaching

A process used for whitening wood, not cloths.

blistering

This is a condition of paint failure where the surface of the finish swells to form blisters. The causes could be entrapped moisture, excessive heat, or improper application.

blueprint

Blueprinting is a process typically used to produce construction drawings. A blueprint has a dark blue background and white lines. Other, more common printing techniques produce black-line and blue-line prints, where the background is white and the lines are black or blue.

board & batten

See "batten."

board foot

A unit of measure for lumber. A board foot is equivalent to a piece of wood 1-foot square x 1-inch thick.

borrow soil

On plans and in specifications, this usually refers to soil that is taken from another location.

borrowed light

This refers to a window that receives secondary light, such as a window in an interior corridor that is illuminated by a skylight--the window is borrowing light from the skylight.

box girder

A structural form in the shape of a box and made up of metal, wood, or concrete.

box gutter

A gutter built into the edge of a roof, usually lined with galvanized metal, tin, or copper.

breezeway

A covered passageway between two structures that is open at each end, or one which passes through a building.

brick

A clay or clay mixture molded into blocks, which are then hardened by baking in a kiln. Brick can be made in a number of earth tones, surface finishes, and shapes. A Standard size brick is 2-1/4" x 3-1/2" x 7 -1/2". Other common bricks sizes, Roman and Norman, are larger.

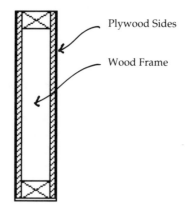

Plywood Sides

Wood Frame

Box Girder

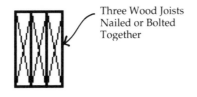

Built-up Wood Beam

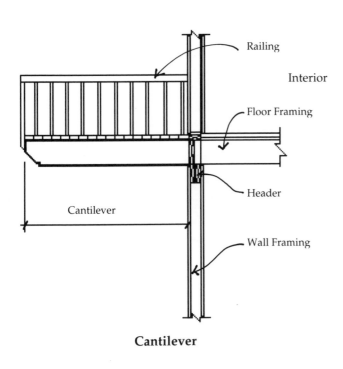

Cantilever

brickbat

Pieces of broken brick.

brick veneer

A brick facing applied to the surface of a frame, or other type, structure.

bridging

Small wooden or metal pieces inserted between floor, wall, or roof framing members to stiffen them.

brownstone

A red-brown sandstone used extensively as a building material in the early 20th century. Also, the name given to row houses built of the material in the northeast U.S.

Btu

British thermal unit is the amount of heat required to raise the temperature of one pound of water one degree Fahrenheit. Almost all heat references on plans and in specifications will be in Btu.

built-up beam

A structural member made up by bolting or nailing two or more wood or metal pieces together.

built-up roof

A roofing system composed of a series of layers of water-proof materials.

bulkhead

Generally, this term will refer to a temporary partition inserted in a concrete form to contain fresh concrete, such as at the end of a form, or at a construction joint.

bull's eye

A circular opening, such as a circular arch or window.

bungalow

A one-story house with low sweeping lines and a wide veranda. Occasionally, the attic space will be finished, but a bungalow is always a single story. Popular in the early part of the 20th century, the style evolved into 1-1/2- and 2-story versions referred to as "bungaloids."

caisson (pile)

A type of foundation pile which is surrounded with concrete. A caisson pile is usually larger than two feet in diameter. A smaller pile is referred to as a pier.

calcimine

A white (or tinted) wash made of whiting and glue mixed with water used to coat wall surfaces.

cant (strip)

When noted on plans, a cant is a sloping piece of lumber used on roofs as a transition from vertical to horizontal surfaces.

cantilever

A structural term referring to a projection supported only at one end.

capillary action

The seepage of moisture through material. In buildings this is sometimes referred to as "rising damp." In historic structures it was prevented by the installation of a water table. In contemporary construction, flashing at the base of a building can stop capillary action.

capital

The upper part of a column or pilaster. The most common classical column capitals are from Greek architecture -- Corinthian, Doric, and Ionic. Roman architecture added two additional styles -- Tuscan and Composite.

carborundum

This is an abrasive made from a combination of carbon and silicon. It is often used in the manufacture of materials to be used as walking surfaces, such as carborundum quarry tile, to provide an abrasive surface.

cased opening

An opening finished with trim, but without a window or door.

casement (window)

A window that is hinged from the side edge.

cast-in-place

This is a term most often used in reference to concrete. It means that the concrete is allowed to harden where it is placed, as opposed to precast concrete.

catch basin

A cistern located at the point where a gutter (street) discharges into a sewer to catch debris. Also, a reservoir to catch and retain surface drainage. On plans, a catch basin will generally be noted just by the letters "CB."

catenary

The curve assumed by a cord or cable hanging freely between two points of support in equilibrium under given forces.

caulk

caulk (v): to drive oakum or other material into joints to make them airtight or watertight.

caulk (n): a mastic substance used to seal exterior joints or edges, such as around windows or doors.

cavity wall

Although this does not mean that the wall needs dental work, it does indicate that there is a void in the wall. This term is generally used when referring to a brick wall made up of two independent columns tied together with metal or brick.

cement

Any material that causes other materials or articles to bind together. In manufacturing concrete, cement would cause the sand and coarse aggregate and steel reinforcing to bind together.

cement mortar

Material composed of Portland cement, sand, and water, but no coarse aggregate.

cement plaster

Gypsum plaster which is prepared to be used as a base-coat plaster.

ceramic tile

A thin piece of fired clay. Ceramic tile can be made in any shape or color, glazed or unglazed, and used on just about any surface -- floors, counters, walls, or ceilings.

cesspool

On plans, this usually refers to a pit used for reception and detention of sewage.

chamfer

A bevel edge formed by cutting away the corner or edge of wood or masonry

channel iron

This is a structural member made up of rolled steel with the sides turned inward.

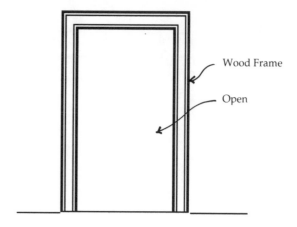

Cased Opening

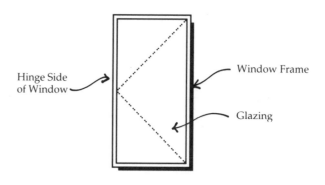

Casement Window

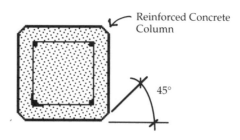

Chamfered Column

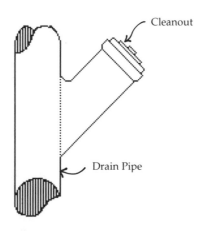

Cleanout

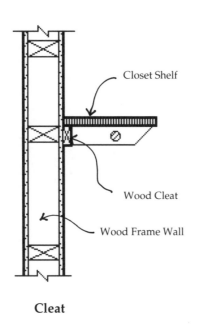

Cleat

chase

A chase is a vertical groove or channel designed to receive pipes, ducts, or conduits. A horizontal channel for the same purpose is referred to as a raceway.

chimney pot

A pipe or clay tile or metal placed at the top of a chimney to improve the draft and carry smoke off. They were used extensively up until the beginning of the 20th century.

cleanout

Usually found on plumbing plans, this term refers to a removable plate or plug providing access to a drainage pipe to allow cleaning. On plans, this will generally be noted just by the letters "CO."

cleat

A strip of wood or metal used for supporting some object.

clerestory

The portion of a multistory room extending above an adjacent lower room. The clerestory space generally contains windows to admit light and ventilation into the taller space.

cob wall

A wall of clay blocks made from unfired clay mixed with straw.

cobwork

Logs laid horizontally with the ends joined so as to form an enclosure.

coffer

When referenced on plans, a coffer is usually an ornamental, recessed panel on a ceiling or soffit.

On structural drawings, a coffer would refer to a structural pan system.

collar beam

A horizontal tie in a roof truss, connecting two opposite rafters.

colonnade

A series of columns at regular intervals.

column

A perpendicular structural member, usually circular, square, or rectangular in shape.

composition roofing

Roofing consisting of asbestos felt saturated with asphalt, and assembled with asphalt cement. Also called roll roofing.

concealed gutter

A gutter constructed in such a manner that it cannot be seen. Also referred to as a "box gutter."

concrete

A mixture of cement, sand, aggregate, and water.

concrete bent

A precast concrete frame where the horizontal load-bearing portion is designed as a cantilever.

concrete block

A hollow or solid precast concrete masonry unit (CMU).

condensate

Any liquid formed by the condensation of vapor.

conduction

The transfer of heat by contact.

conduit

On plans and in specifications, a conduit is a stiff tube or pipe designed to carry electrical wires.

construction joint

A rigid joint where two sections of a structure are joined to form a continuous plane or mass.

contour

On site plans a contour illustrates a level or elevation of ground relative to some constant level, such as sea level.

control joint

A groove cut or tooled into concrete, plaster, or stucco in an effort to predetermine the location of cracks caused by shrinkage. The most common control joints are those found in concrete sidewalks.

cooling tower

This refers to a device used for cooling water used in air-conditioning condensers. A cooling tower will generally be located outside -- adjacent to a structure or, most often, on the roof of a building.

coping

This is the cap or top course of a masonry wall.

corbelling

A construction method of stepping masonry construction up and out from a building wall. This detail is often found at the cornice line of Victorian period structures.

Corinthian Order

The most ornate of the Greek orders of architecture.

cornice

A cornice can take many forms. It is the construction where the roof and side walls meet, or the top course of a wall when treated as a crowning member.

corrugated iron

When noted on plans or in specifications, corrugated iron refers to sheet metal, usually galvanized, used either as a form for concrete floors, or as a wall or roof covering.

course

A course is a continuous level row of brick or stone.

cove molding

A concave quarter-round molding.

CPM

Critical Path Method of scheduling. This is the most common method of scheduling construction projects. It establishes a list of activities that must occur in a specific sequence to complete the project within a fixed time frame.

crawl space

Th e space under a building between the first floor and the ground surface.

crazing

The minute cracking of a finish coat of paint or masonry surface. This is generally caused by uneven shrinkage.

crest (cresting)

A decorative ridging of a roof.

cricket

A small elevated part of a roof designed to act as a watershed.

crown

The uppermost member of the cornice, or the high point in sidewalk or road construction.

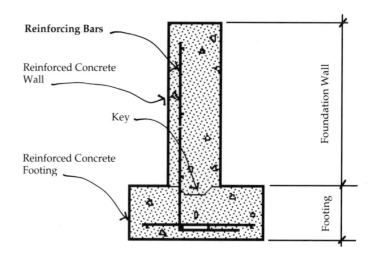

Concrete Foundation

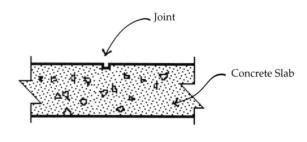

Control Joint

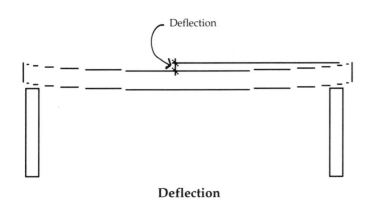

Deflection

Deflection

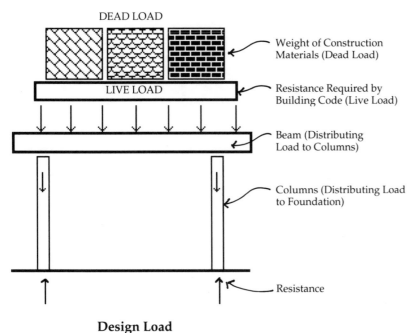

DEAD LOAD

Weight of Construction Materials (Dead Load)

LIVE LOAD

Resistance Required by Building Code (Live Load)

Beam (Distributing Load to Columns)

Columns (Distributing Load to Foundation)

Resistance

Design Load

crown molding

The molding at the top of the cornice, immediately beneath the roof or ceiling .

CRSI

Abbreviation for the Concrete Reinforcing Steel Institute.

CSI

Construction Specifications Institute. (See the "Specifications" chapter of this book for CSI formats.)

curtain wall

A thin wall applied to a steel or concrete building frame.

datum point

A point of elevation used as a reference by which levels and distances are measured. This would appear on a benchmark on a site plan.

decibel

A unit of sound measurement.

deflection

In structural terms, a deflection is the bending of a beam or any part of a structure under an applied load.

deformed bar

A standard type of steel reinforcing bar used in concrete construction. A deformed bar is made with ridges to produce a better bond between the steel reinforcing and concrete.

dentil

In the Corinthian Order of Greek architecture, a cog or tooth used in the entablature.

design load

This is the load for which structural members are designed, such as a floor being designed to withstand 100 pounds of weight per square foot. When indicated on mechanical drawings, a design load generally refers to the capacity required of an air-conditioning or heating system to produce and maintain specified conditions. In these cases it may be cited as Btu or tons of air conditioning.

dew point

This is the point at which dew begins to form.

dimension lumber

Lumber that is milled to specific dimensions, generally under 4" x 16".

divided light

A window divided into small panes of glass.

door jamb

The side frame upon which a door hinges or latches. The door head will generally appear the same in detail as the jambs.

door schedule

On architectural plans, a listing which identifies all doors in a building, providing location, type, size, operation, and finish.

door sill

The detail at the bottom of a door opening upon which a door stops. Also known as the threshold.

Doric Order

In Greek architectural orders, Doric is the earliest and simplest form.

dormer (window)

A vertical projection built out from a sloping roof or an extension of the exterior wall above a roof line. A dormer usually contains a window, thus dormer window.

double-hung window

A window that has an upper and a lower sash which both slide up and down.

In a single-hung window, just one sash (usually the lower) operates.

draftsman's scale

A measuring scale used in creating drawings. Architects use scales divided into inches; engineers often use scales divided by centimeters.

dry rubble

Rough stone placed in a wall without mortar.

drywall

Sheets of gypsum board used as an interior finish, also referred to as wallboard.

drywell

A pit, usually lined with masonry, designed to allow liquid effluent to leach or percolate into the soil.

ducts

Pipes or tubes, round or rectangular, designed to distribute air in a heating, ventilating or air-conditioning system.

Dutch door

A door that is divided horizontally, allowing the lower portion to be closed while the upper portion remains open.

dutchman

An odd piece of woodwork inserted to fill an opening or to correct a defect.

eaves

The portion of roof that extends over the exterior wall.

efflorescence

Generally seen on brick walls, this is a white, powdery substance caused by calcium carbide leeching through the masonry. Although it can be washed off, it will usually continue to return until the minerals are depleted.

engaged columns

Columns that are embedded or attached to a wall.

English bond

A brick bond in which one course is made up entirely of headers, and the next course entirely of stretchers. The header and stretcher courses alternate throughout the wall.

entablature

That portion of a building that rests horizontally on columns and consists of a cornice, frieze, and architrave.

escutcheon

The shield placed around a light switch, keyhole, light fixture outlet, etc., to protect the adjacent finish.

evaporative cooler

An air-conditioning system which draws cooler air through moisture and then circulates it through a building. This system is used extensively in low-humidity regions.

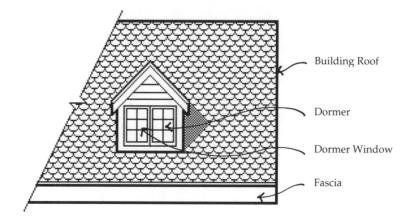

Dormer Window

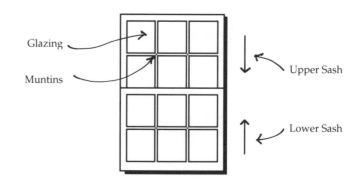

Double-hung Window

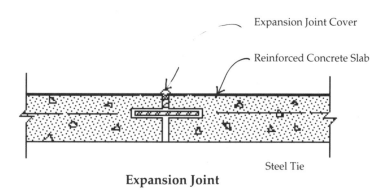

Expansion Joint

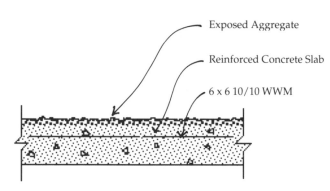

Exposed Aggregate Concrete

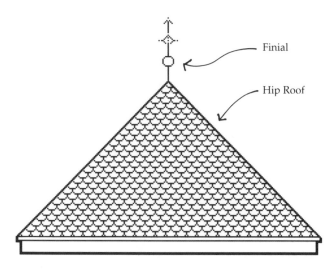

Finial on a Folly

expansion joint

In structural systems, an expansion joint is a flexible connection between two portions of a structure.

exposed aggregate

A concrete finish where the coarse aggregate is exposed on the surface.

facade

The entire exterior surface of a building, especially the front.

face brick

Historically, a better quality brick used on the public face of a building. At times, the face brick would be different sizes, shapes, or patterns.

face putty

The glazing putty that is placed in the angle of the sash after the glass is laid.

fascia

A long, flat member in the entablature, or at the edge of a beam, used as a finish, nonstructural, element.

feathering

When noted on plans or in specifications, this refers to flattening out the edges of a material to blend it with new material, such as feathering the edges of existing paint to blend with new paint.

fenestration

The arrangement of openings in a facade.

fillet

As a structural reference, a fillet is the concave junction formed when two structural members meet. It is normally used as a welding term.

finial

An ornamental device capping a gable or spire.

finish coat

A reference used in both plaster work and painting. In both cases it refers to the final (finish) coat of material.

finish floor

This notation can be found on plans as an elevation reference. On floor plans, sections, elevations, and details, the term will be noted "fin fl" and usually be the point from which something is measured, such as 36" above fin fl. This means that the object would be located 36 inches above the final floor elevation.

finish grade

This refers to the final surface elevation of elements outside of the structure, such as planted areas, roadways, and sidewalks.

fire barriers

On architectural plans, this would refer to any obstruction to prevent the spread of fire, such as a fire door or stair enclosure.

firebrick

A type of brick that is made especially for use in high-heat locations, such as fireplaces. It is made of a different material than standard construction brick.

fire cut

An angle cut at the end of a floor joist where it is anchored in a masonry wall; designed to prevent displacement of the wall in case the wood joist should collapse.

fire door

A door that is made of fire-resistant material. A fire door will be rated by Underwriters Laboratory to resist burning for a specified period of time--3/4 of an hour, 1 hour, 2 hours, 4 hours.

fire escape

Usually, an exterior-applied steel or wood ladder designed to provide a means of escape from a building during a fire.

fire wall

A wall built to restrict or contain fire, preventing it from spreading to other parts of a building or to another structure.

flashing

Metal or plastic strips of film installed to prevent water penetration through joints, such as over windows and doors and between exterior walls and roofing.

Flemish bond

A brick bond consisting of alternating headers and stretchers in each course.

floated coat

The second coat of plaster, applied over the scratch coat.

floor plan

A graphic representation of the floor pattern of a building. On drawings, a floor plan is a view looking downward from five feet above the floor. A set of drawings would normally have a separate floor plan for each level of a structure. (*See* "The Drawings" chapter of this book.)

flue

On plans and in specifications, a flue is an enclosed passageway, round or rectangular, such as a pipe or chimney, designed to carry off fumes or smoke.

flush valve

This is a reference found on plumbing drawings and in specifications meaning a valve used to flush water through a plumbing fixture, such as a water closet.

footing

Eliminate the word "footer" from your vocabulary: it is a "footing." A structural term meaning a form used to spread or distribute the load of a wall over a wide area. It is sometimes referred to as a "spread footing" when it extends along the length of the wall. When it is located directly under a free-standing column, it might be referred to as a "pad."

foundation

That portion of a structure upon which the superstructure is erected. The foundation can consist of footings, foundation walls, piling, and other support elements below the ground.

foundation wall

Any structural wall below the first floor joists or beams.

framing

The skeleton parts of a building, such as wood floor and roof joists and stud walls.

freeze-thaw cycle

The cycle of freezing, thawing, freezing, thawing.

French door

Doors with glazed panels extending the full length of the door, usually hung in pairs.

fresco

The process of painting on wet plaster.

frost line

The maximum depth to which the earth will freeze. Footings should be located at or below the frost line. This depth varies depending on the geographic location of the construction site.

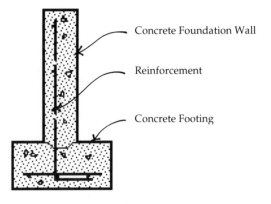

Spread Footing

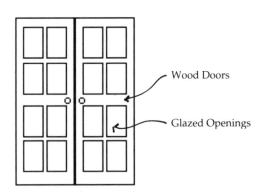

French Doors

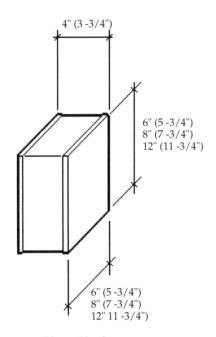

4" (3 -3/4")

6" (5 -3/4")
8" (7 -3/4")
12" (11 -3/4")

6" (5 -3/4")
8" (7 -3/4")
12" 11 -3/4")

Glass Block

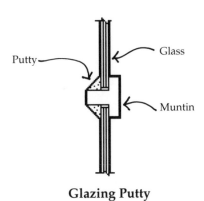

Putty

Glass

Muntin

Glazing Putty

furring

The process of leveling a portion of a floor, wall, or ceiling.

furring strips

Flat pieces of wood used to level uneven framing or placed against a masonry wall to facilitate the placement of a finished wall material.

fusible link

A mechanism used as part of a hold-open device on a fire door or screen that breaks or melts when subjected to heat, allowing the fire door or screen to close.

galvanizing

The process of applying a coat of zinc to metal. This is done to prevent rusting.

Georgian style

An architectural style popular in England during the reign of the Georges (1714-1830). This style was popular in America in the mid-1700s.

German siding

A type of wood siding with the upper part of the exposed face finished with a concave curve, and the lower portion of the back rabbeted.

gingerbread

Ornate detailing used on houses during the later part of the 19th century and early 20th century.

girder

A large horizontal structural member used to support walls or floors.

glass block

A hollow, non-structural glass form.

glaze

The process of installing glass in openings, such as in windows or doors.

Gothic architecture

The style prevalent in western Europe from the 12th through 16th centuries.

grading

The process of filling in around a structure with earth.

groin

On plans, this would refer to the intersection of two vaults.

grout

A fluid cement mixture used to fill crevices.

gutter

A horizontal channel of wood, metal, or plastic designed to carry off water from a roof area.

gypsum wallboard

See "drywall."

hardboard

A pressed-wood panel.

H beam

A structural member in the shape of an "H" made of rolled steel.

header

Header has a number of possible meanings when used on plans and in specifications. In brick construction, it is a brick laid so its small side faces outward and it extends back into the wall. As a structural member, a header is usually a built-up beam designed to transfer joist or rafter loads. In wall framing, headers are used over window and door openings to support the walls above the openings.

herringbone

A pattern of laying masonry or wood forming a zigzag, with the end of one piece laid at right angles to the side of another.

high-early-strength cement

A type of Portland cement known as Type III, which hardens and reaches its full strength faster than other types of cement.

hip

The exterior angle formed by the intersection of two sloping sides of a roof.

hood mold

A projecting molding over the head of a window or door opening, designed as a decoration.

hopper window

A window type which opens inward on hinges at the bottom of the sash.

hydraulic mortar

A type of mortar that hardens under water.

hydraulic pressure

In architecture, this term usually refers to water pressure found under concrete slabs.

insulation

Any material designed to prevent heat transmission. Insulation can come in the form of blankets, batts, boards, or loose material. Also, insulation can refer to the protective coating over electrical wire.

Ionic Order

A style of Greek architecture typified by a scroll detail as a decoration element on column capitals.

isometric drawing

A drawing where all horizontal lines are drawn at 30°, all vertical lines are drawn vertically, and all dimensions are accurate on the 30°-angle lines and the vertical lines.

jack arch

An arch which is flat instead of curved, rounded, or pointed.

jib door

A door which continues the plane and general appearance of the adjacent wall or window.

joist

The wood structural member designed to support floors or ceiling finishes (floor joists, ceiling joists).

Keene's cement

A white, very hard, finish plaster.

keystone

A structural, wedge-shaped piece of material at the center of an arch, which serves to lock all of the arch pieces together.

laminated arches

Arched structural members made up of thin strips of wood glued or nailed together, allowing the beams to span great distances, while being aesthetically pleasing.

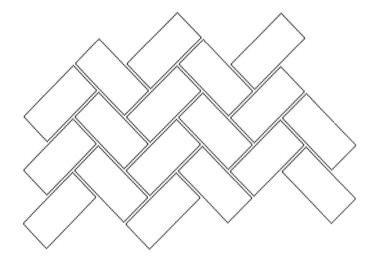

Herringbone Pattern

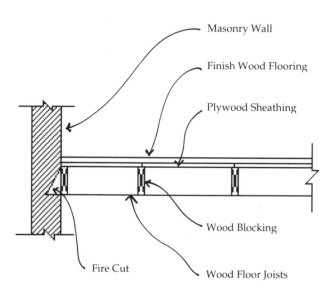

Masonry Wall

Finish Wood Flooring

Plywood Sheathing

Wood Blocking

Fire Cut

Wood Floor Joists

**Section Thru Wood
Floor Framing**

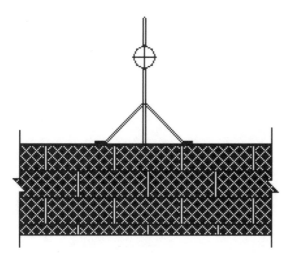

Lightning Rod

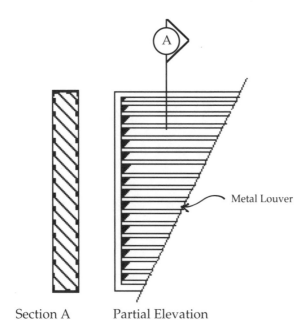

Section A   Partial Elevation

Metal Louver

Louver

lanai

A covered walkway; Hawaiian for "porch."

lantern

A cupola, or crowning architectural element, located on top of a roof and designed to give light and air to an interior space.

lath

Metal mesh or wooden strips used as a base for plaster.

lean-to

Generally a small structure built as an addition to a larger building and having a single-sloped roof whose roof rafters "lean" against the other building.

level

A tool, also known as a "spirit level," used to determine if an object or line is parallel or perpendicular to the force of gravity.

lightning rod

A metal rod extending from the highest point of a building or structure to the ground, protecting the building from damage by lightning.

lintel

A structural member, made up of wood or metal, placed horizontally across the top of an opening, such as a window or door. The lintel will generally be at least four inches longer than the width of the opening.

live load

In designing the structural elements of a building, live load represents the anticipated weight of the activity to be carried out in the building. Live loads are established by building code and will vary in accordance with building use. For example, a residential structure is usually designed to withstand 40 pounds of weight per square foot of floor area, while the stack area in a library is designed for 150 pounds per square foot load. The required live load, plus the weight of the construction materials themselves, referred to as the "dead load," represents the design load of a building. (*See* design load.)

lookout

A short structural member used to support the overhang of a roof.

louver

A slatted opening, designed to provide ventilation.

mansard roof

A roof form developed for use in France and used extensively by the architect Francois Mansart (1598-1666). It is a roof with two slopes, the uppermost, almost flat, and the lower slope, very steep. It was developed originally to house an additional floor in a building without appearing to be another story higher.

masonry

A generic term applied to anything constructed of stone, brick, tile, concrete, or other similar materials.

metal ties

This is a term used for any type of lightweight steel ties used to join or bond separate elements of masonry wall construction.

modulus of elasticity

This is a term used in structural design representing the ratio of normal stress to corresponding strain for tensile or compression stresses below the proportional limit of the material. In other words, if the stress on a structural member exceeds the modulus of elasticity of the material, you've got trouble.

mortar

In historic buildings, a pasty material composed of sand and lime. In contemporary construction, a mixture of cement, sand, and water. (Contemporary mortar should not be used in historic buildings and vice-versa.)

mortar joints

The joints between masonry units filled with mortar. Mortar joints can be finished in different shapes-- flush, struck, concave, V, beaded, and many more.

newel post

The primary post at the foot of a stairway or at a landing, supporting the string and handrail.

oakum

Hemp or rope used for packing caulking joints.

o/c

On Center, when used on plans or in specifications, is a measurement from the centerline of one element to the centerline of another, for instance, "#3ø 6" o/c ea. way" means 3/8" round reinforcing bars placed 6" in each direction.

offset

This is a reference on plans referring to a change in the plane of a surface.

ogee arch

An arch which has a compound curve, part concave and part convex.

open-web steel joists

This generally refers to a composite structural element made up of light steel members.

orders of architecture

The much used and misused orders of architecture are: from the Greek -- Doric, Ionic, and Corinthian; and from the Roman -- Tuscan and Composite.

OSHA

Occupational Safety and Health Act.

pan floor

A flooring system made up of a series of interconnecting concrete beams joined together at the top with a thin concrete slab.

parapet wall

The portion of an exterior building wall, party wall, or fire wall, which extends above the roof line.

parging

A thin coat of cement plaster used to smooth masonry surfaces.

particle board

A composite made up of wood fibers bonded together to form panels.

partition

Usually an interior wall used to separate spaces of a building. These can be constructed of any material, be permanent or temporary, stationary or portable.

pediment

In classical architecture, a pediment is a triangular element, resembling a gable end of a roof, crowning the entrance of a structure, doorway, or window.

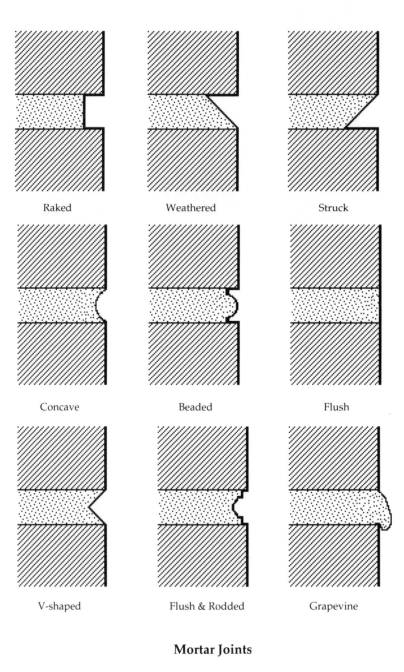

Raked   Weathered   Struck

Concave   Beaded   Flush

V-shaped   Flush & Rodded   Grapevine

Mortar Joints

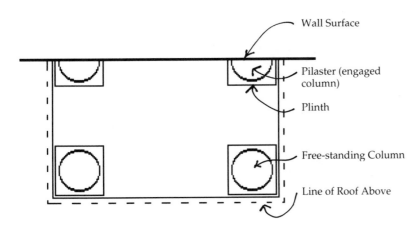

Labels: Wall Surface, Pilaster (engaged column), Plinth, Free-standing Column, Line of Roof Above

Free-standing Columns and Pilasters

penny (d)

The term "penny," when used on plans and in specifications, once referred to the cost (English) of nails per hundred. Penny, abbreviated as "d," now refers to nail size. A 4d nail is approximately 1-1/4" long, a 6d is 2", an 8d is 2-1/2", and so forth.

penthouse

This is a reference to a room located on the roof of a building. A penthouse can house a living space, such as an apartment, or can contain mechanical equipment, such as air conditioners or elevator machinery.

pergola

A structure open to the sky, with its roof constructed of open rafters.

perspective

An illustration of an object on a plane surface so it will have the same appearance as when it is viewed from a particular location.

A perspective drawing of a building or a structure basically shows the building as it would look in real life. There are one-point perspectives, where all the horizontal lines spring from a single point. Generally, one-point perspectives are used on drawings of interiors. There are two-point perspectives, with two vanishing points. This technique is used on most exterior renderings of buildings. And, there are three-point perspectives, not often used and quite complicated.

piazza

An enclosed courtyard, arcade, or colonnade of a building.

pier

As a structural element, a wood, masonry, steel, or concrete column or isolated foundation member used to support foundations, floors, or walls.

In architectural work, an element supporting an arch or section of a wall over an opening.

pilaster

A round, square, or rectangular column attached to a wall.

pile

A wood, steel, precast or prestressed concrete shaft driven into the ground for support of a structure.

pitch

In architectural terms, pitch refers to the slope of roof rafters, expressed as a ratio of rise to run. On drawings, it will either be noted as slope per inch on roof plans, or illustrated as a small triangle on elevation drawings.

In plumbing, pitch is the slope of a surface to a drain.

plaster

Historically, a mixture of lime, sand, water, and a fiber (usually animal hair) made to form a thick, pasty mortar used to cover walls and ceilings.

plaster grounds

Strips or pieces of wood nailed to walls to serve as guides for plastering. Also used as nailing strips for finish material, such as trim and moldings.

plate

On architectural drawings the word "plate" can refer to the topmost, horizontal wood member in a frame wall. It can also reference the wood member placed at the top of a foundation wall onto which the floor framing members are attached.

plate glass

A thick, smooth, high-grade glass historically used for glazing large openings.

plenum

Plenum is a term found on mechanical drawings, referring to a pressurized air chamber connecting two or more air-distribution ducts.

plinth

The square base of a column, wall, or frame.

plot plan

Historically, a plot plan illustrated the plot of land upon which a building was to be constructed. A more contemporary set of drawings will refer to a "plot" as a "site," thus -- a "site plan."

plumb bob

A weight attached to a line, used in surveying to establish a point or line.

plywood

A widely used building material which is made up of two or more thin sheets of wood glued together with the grain of adjacent layers at right angles to each other.

plywood grades

Plywood is graded for different kinds of use and exposure. If it is marked "exterior," waterproof glue was used to bind the sheets of wood together. Otherwise, it would be used only in areas that are not subject to exposure to moisture. The finish of the plywood is rated in letters--A, B, or C, with A grade being a smooth, knot-free surface. B and C grades are of lesser quality. The grading you will see on plywood might read "Exterior A-C," which means that it is exterior grade, with one surface finished in A-grade wood, and the other in C-grade wood.

pointing

On plans and in specifications, this refers to finishing the joints in brick and stone walls.

porch

A covered entrance or extension to a building, a type of enclosed veranda.

Portland cement

A hydraulic cement consisting of silica, lime, and alumina -- mixed and then ground into a fine powder. This is then used in making concrete by mixing the cement with sand, a coarse aggregate such as gravel, and water.

post and beam construction

A type of construction where posts and beams are the primary load-bearing elements.

post-tensioned concrete

A structural system by which wires or cables are run through either precast or monolithic concrete and placed in tension.

precast concrete

Both architectural and structural elements that usually are cast off-site, shipped to the construction site, and erected. Precast concrete units can be columns, beams, sections of walls, or roofs.

prefabricated

In construction this can refer to building components, such as walls or roof sections, constructed in a factory and brought to the site. It may also reference interior finish elements like cabinet work or "prehung" doors.

prehung doors

Doors that are brought to a construction site already attached to their frame.

preservative

A substance applied to or injected into wood to protect it from damage from moisture, fungi, or insects.

pressed brick

This is a product that was used extensively in the later part of the 19th century and early 20th century. It is a brick which is molded to form a special surface finish or pattern.

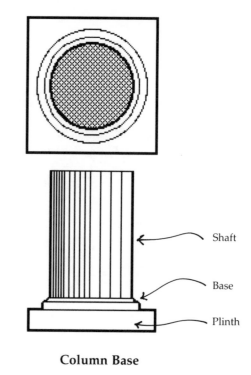

Shaft

Base

Plinth

Column Base

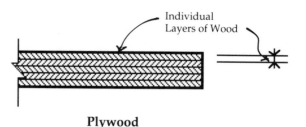

Individual Layers of Wood

Plywood

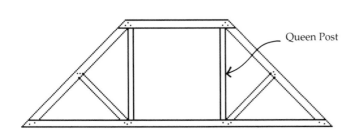

Queen Brick

Corner Brick
Cut Square

Standard Brick Bond

Wood Truss w/ Queen Posts

Queen Post

primer

The first coat of paint applied to a surface.

property line

This is a reference found on site plans. It identifies the limit of the property.

purlins

These are secondary structural members installed as horizontal beams in roof construction.

putty

Historically, a type of cement made up of whiting and linseed oil, used to seal glass in window sash, sometimes referred to as "face putty," or "glazing."

PVC

PVC stands for polyvinyl chloride. It is a material used in the manufacturing of piping used in mechanical and electrical work.

quarry tile

An unglazed tile, usually earth tones in color.

quartersawn wood

A piece of wood cut lengthwise into quarters, with the saw cut parallel with the medullary rays of the wood.

queen closure

A piece of brick cut lengthwise and inserted to end or close a brick corner.

queen post

Vertical ties in a roof truss.

quoins

Quoins, which can most often be found in Georgian architecture, are large stones, or simulated stones, at the outside corners of masonry buildings.

rabbet

This is a term used in woodworking which refers to a groove cut in the surface or edge of a piece of wood to receive another board.

raceway

A horizontal channel used to run electrical or mechanical lines. A vertical channel is called a "chase."

rafter

A structural member in roof framing which extends from the ridge of the roof to the eaves.

rain water leader

A pipe which conveys water from the roof to the ground. Also referred to as a "downspout."

raked joint

In masonry construction, a joint in which the mortar is "raked" out to a specific depth.

raking

The construction method of stepping masonry up and in to the building wall. This detail is most often found at the base of Victorian period structures.

rebar

Slang for reinforcement bar.

receptacle

On electrical plans and in specifications, this refers to the device, such as a wall plug, placed in an outlet box.

reeding

An architectural and woodworking term that applies to molding which resembles reeds. Reeding will most often be found on columns.

reinforced concrete

Concrete in which steel reinforcing bars are embedded to provide tensile strength.

reinforcing

The steel bars used to reinforce concrete.

relieving arch

Any element built over an opening to relieve or distribute weight or loads.

rendering

This is a term used to describe a delineation of a building plan, elevation, or perspective that simulates real settings, textures, and landscape.

retaining wall

A structural element designed to hold back, or retain, earth or other lateral pressure.

retarder (retarding agent)

An admixture used in concrete construction or mortar to slow or "retard" setting.

reveal

In architectural drawings and woodworking, a reveal refers to a recessed space between building materials.

Richardsonian Romanesque

A style of architecture named after the late 19th- and early 20th-century American architect Henry Hobson Richardson.

ridge pole

A horizontal structural member at the top, or ridge, of a roof which receives the upper ends of roof joists.

ridge ventilator

A horizontal raised section of a roof ridge used to exhaust heated air.

right-hand door

Door swings have been a mystery to most architects and non-architects for years. There are four possible swings --right-hand, right-hand reverse, left-hand, and left-hand reverse. The way you determine which is to look at the door from what would be the outside. If the door hinges are on the right side of the door, it's a right-hand door. Then imagine yourself standing with your back against the hinge side. If a right-hand door swings to the left, it is a right-hand reverse door. If it swings to the right it is a right-hand door. The same system can be used on left-hand doors. If the door swings to the left, it is a left-hand door, if to the right, it is a left-hand reverse.

riprap

Masonry or concrete laid randomly against earth to form a barrier.

rise

The vertical distance between a roof plate and the ridge, or the height of a stair.

riser

The vertical face under a stair tread.

Rococo

An ornate style of architecture prevalent briefly in Europe during the 17th and 18th centuries.

Roman brick

A solid masonry unit 2" x 4" x 12".

Romanesque architecture

A style of architecture used in western Europe immediately before the Gothic style. The most dominate element of Romanesque architecture is the rounded arch.

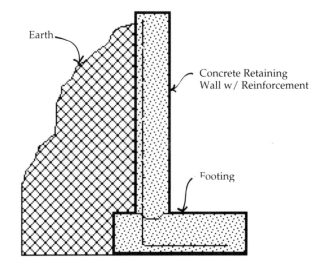

Retaining Wall

roof

The exterior, structural, overhead covering of a building.

roofing

The material covering a roof.

roof pitch

A roof pitch is the slope of the roof surface. On drawings, this will be shown as a fraction representing the rise of the roof over its span.

roof sheathing

Plywood or wood boards nailed to roof rafters to form a solid, flat surface over which roofing is placed.

roof truss

A structural element made up of light wood or steel members assembled to form a roof support.

rose window

An ornamental circular window decorated with roselike tracery and mullions radiating from the center.

rough coat

The first coat of plaster applied to a wall or ceiling surface.

roughing-in

This is a common term used to represent the first, or rough, as opposed to the finished carpentry, plaster, or plumbing work.

rowlock

A course of brick laid on its side.

rubble

In masonry construction, rubble is broken stones or brick used to fill walls.

rung

A horizontal bar connecting two sides of a ladder.

running bond

A course of brick laid on its bottom.

rustication

When used on drawings and in specifications, this term refers to a stone with a rough surface.

saddle

In construction, this has nothing to do with horses. A saddle is the ridge covering of a roof.

salamander

Temporary heating unit used on construction sites to maintain temperatures in enclosed spaces.

sandstone

Used extensively in the late 19th and early 20th centuries, sandstone is a relatively soft stone composed of fine grains of sand bonded with silica, oxide of iron, or carbonate of lime.

sash

The frame in which window panes are placed.

scagliola

An imitation of ornamental marble used primarily on interior surfaces.

scarf joint

An overlapping, notched joint between two pieces of timber.

screed

In concrete or plasterwork, a screed is the wood or metal edge used to strike the level of a slab or wall.

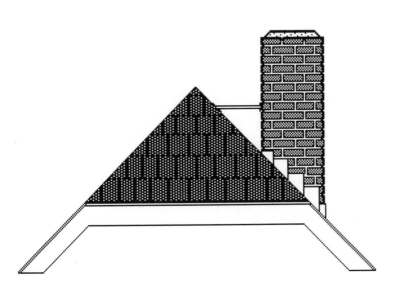

Jerkinheaded Roof

scribe

To mark or rule a line on wood or other material with a sharp instrument.

sealant

On drawings and in specifications, this will usually refer to a clear coating applied to wood, masonry, or concrete to prevent moisture penetration.

section

On drawings, a section generally refers to a vertical cut through a building or site illustrating all or a portion of that element.

segmented arch

A masonry arch where the arc is less than a semicircle.

septic tank

A concrete tank used to hold sewage during the process of disintegration by bacteria.

setback

This is a term found on site plans. It refers to the distance a structure is set back from a property line. The minimum setback is established by local zoning and building codes.

shaft

On plans and in specifications, the word "shaft" can have two meanings. On architectural drawings, it will refer to the center portion of a column, that section extending from the base to the capital. On mechanical drawings, a shaft is a vertical opening through which air-distribution ducts will run.

shear

This is a structural term referring to a failure caused by the meeting of opposite forces. Shear can be either perpendicular or parallel, and can occur in wood, steel, or concrete.

shear wall

A structural element designed to withstand shear forces caused by wind or earthquakes.

sheathing

Sheathing is usually a wood membrane applied as a covering for roofs, exterior walls, and floors.

shed roof

A roof form having one slope.

shim

This is a thin piece of material, wood, or metal, used as a level or fill in construction.

shingle

A thin piece of wood, stone, or composition material used as a roof or wall covering. Shingles can be manufactured in any number of forms and shapes.

Hand-split wood shingles are referred to as "shakes."

shoe

In construction, a shoe is part of the finish wood trim in a building. It is the quarter round located at the bottom of a wood base, making a transition between the floor and wall.

shoring

Usually a temporary installation of timber, steel, or concrete members placed to retain earth or water.

shotcreting

The spray placement of concrete at high velocity. This system is most often used in swimming pool construction.

siding

An exterior finish on a building, generally wood.

sill

Sill is a term which can be used in many different locations on a set of drawings. It will usually refer to the lowest member under a window or door. It can also reference the lowest member supporting a frame structure.

skim coat

This is a thin, finishing coat of plaster.

skylight

On plans and in specifications, a skylight will refer to a window or covering fitting into or over an opening in a roof for admitting daylight.

slab

This is a structural term referring to a flat area of concrete. A slab may be placed directly on earth or can be part of a larger structural system, such as columns, beams, and slab.

sleeper

Generally, the term sleeper will be found on architectural drawings and refer to strips of wood laid over a rough slab to which a finished wood floor is attached.

slipform

This is a method of construction where the concrete form moves continuously. It is not a very common method of construction because of the precision required.

slope

Slope can be used in reference to many different building systems on a project, but will always refer to the incline of an object, such as a roof, floor, or site.

slump

In specifications and in concrete construction, slump is a measurement of the relative stiffness of a concrete mix. Concrete specifications may call for a slump of 3" to 5". To measure this, a contractor will fill a 12"-high metal cone with fresh concrete as it arrives at the construction site. After proper preparation, the cone will be lifted up quickly and the height of the resulting concrete pile will be measured. Its height must be within 3" to 5" inches of the original 12" height. If it is less than three inches, the concrete is too stiff and may require additional water (which should never be added at the site). If the slump is greater than five inches, it is too wet and unusable.

smoke chamber

In fireplace construction, a smoke chamber is the slanted area immediately above the smoke shelf and damper.

smoke shelf

A projection at the bottom of the smoke chamber designed to prevent downdrafts from forcing smoke into a room.

soffit

The underside of any subordinate member in a structure, such as an arch, cornice, eaves, or stair.

soil pipe

A soil pipe carries waste matter from a water closet to the drainage system in a building.

soldier course

In brick construction, this is a course of bricks laid so that they are standing on end.

sole plate

The lowest horizontal member of a wall in frame construction, to which the wall studs are nailed.

spackle

The miracle material for building repairs. Spackle is a flexible plaster used for patching walls and ceilings.

spall

This can be a noun or a verb. A spall is a chip or piece of stone, brick, or concrete broken off a larger element. Having something spall is to have it break or fall away in fragments.

span

The distance between supports.

spandrel

On drawings and in specifications, the term "spandrel" will generally refer to that portion of a wall between the head of one window and the sill of another.

spandrel beam

A horizontal structural member on an exterior wall that forms a spandrel.

specifications

Specifications for a project are part of the contract and construction documents. They are the written instructions to the contractor on the scope of work to be done, the material to be used, and the method by which the work is to be carried out.

spiral stairs

A staircase, circular in plan, made up entirely of winders (wedge-shaped steps).

spread footings

In contemporary terms, a spread footing is one that spreads the weight of a building across a large area of earth.

spring line

A line across the span of an arch passing through the points where the arch is tangent to the vertical plane.

sprinkler system

On mechanical drawings and in specifications for mechanical work, a sprinkler system is a series of water lines inside a building that are designed to release a spray of water through sprinkler heads to extinguish a fire.

On site plans, a sprinkler system would refer to an irrigation system.

stack

On architectural drawings, this is a chimney made of brick, stone, concrete, or metal and is designed to exhaust smoke or fumes from a furnace.

On mechanical drawings, a stack would refer to a soil or vent piping system.

stained glass

A glass that is painted or stained with designs or images. This method was used extensively in the United States up until 1915. After that date most "stained glass" was actually leaded glass. In leaded glass the design or pattern is made up primarily of pieces of colored glass set in lead caming. Both types of glass may be referred to as "art glass."

stair (stairway)

A series of horizontal and vertical elements assembled in a manner to connect one floor or area with another above or below.

stair tread

The horizontal surface connecting risers in a stair.

stiffener

On structural drawings, a stiffener is a member added to strengthen a joint or to prevent buckling of a member or part of a building.

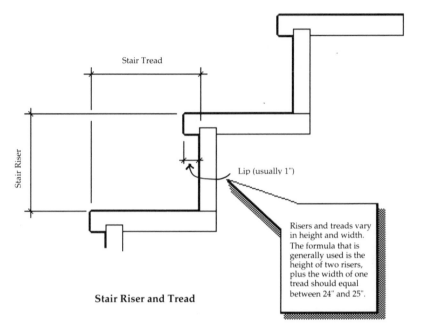

Stair Tread

Stair Riser

Lip (usually 1")

Risers and treads vary in height and width. The formula that is generally used is the height of two risers, plus the width of one tread should equal between 24" and 25".

Stair Riser and Tread

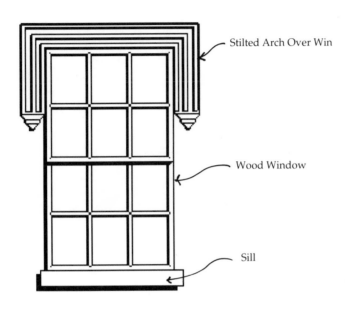

Labels on image: Stilted Arch Over Win, Wood Window, Sill

Stilted Arch

stile

One of the vertical members in a door or window sash into which secondary members are fitted or attached.

stilted arch

An arch having its spring line above the apparent impost.

stirrup

On structural plans, a stirrup is a bent reinforcing bar used to hold the primary reinforcing in place.

stool

In carpentry, the stool is the interior wood base at the bottom of a window.

stoop

A raised platform leading into a building.

storm window

A second window placed on the outside or inside of the primary window, designed to conserve energy by creating a dead air space, and to protect the window.

stretcher

In brickwork, a stretcher is brick laid lengthwise.

stringer

This term will be found primarily on architectural plans as a reference to the inclined member in a stair designed to support the risers and treads.

structural clay tile (SCT)

Hollow masonry units made of clay or shale.

structure

Generally, the term "structure" will be inclusive -- defining an edifice constructed of parts arranged and fitted together.

strut

A structural term used for any piece of material designed and placed to keep two pieces apart, absorbing pressure or stress, such as in a truss.

stucco

Generally, a rough plaster used for exterior coverings on walls.

stud

In a building, a stud is a vertical member used in the framework of a wall. A stud can be made of wood or metal. Unless noted otherwise, on architectural plans a wood stud will be a 2 x 4, measuring 1-9/16" x 3-1/2".

subcontractor

Construction of a building will usually be undertaken by a general contractor. This individual will hire a series of subcontractors to execute specific parts of the project, such as site work, electrical, mechanical, roofing, etc.

subfloor

On architectural plans and in specifications, subfloor refers to the rough boards or plywood placed between the building's structural support (floor joists) and finished floor. It acts as a base for the finished floor and a stiffener for the structure.

sump

A pit or hole in a building where water is allowed to accumulate. These are generally found in buildings where an interior floor elevation is below the level of a sewer or adjacent ground water.

sump pump

A pump used to remove the water allowed to accumulate in the sump.

survey

An accurate measure of the physical properties of a building and/or building site. In a set of drawings there could be a number of different surveys individually shown or combined onto one drawing. There may be a boundary survey showing the property lines and setback requirements; a topographical survey showing the land contours; and, a landscape survey showing all plant material on the site.

suspended ceiling

A ceiling suspended from a structural ceiling above. Contemporary usage generally defines a suspended ceiling as one made up of acoustic-tile panels. The term is correctly used for suspended ceilings of any material--plaster, wood, wallboard, glass, or acoustic panels.

tail cut

The cut on the lower end of a rafter, sometimes to give a decorative effect.

take off

A list of materials and quantities from a set of plans and specifications used for preparation of construction bids.

tamp

The compression of loose soil around a structure by repeatedly pounding it down.

tensile strength

The strength of a material to resist pulling strain.

terra cotta

A fired clay material historically used as decorative tile coverings on building exteriors.

terrazzo

A type of marble mosaic in which cement is used as a matrix and marble chips as coarse aggregate. Once a slab made up of this material is poured and cured, the top surface is ground down to expose the marble chips and polished.

thermostat

An electric or electronic instrument used to measure and regulate air temperature.

three-way switch

On electrical drawings this term, or corresponding symbol, will refer to a switch which allows a circuit to be activated from two different locations.

threshold

A plate under a door.

tie rod

An iron or steel rod used to hold structural elements or parts together.

tile

As used on architectural plans and in specifications, this term refers to a fired clay, stone, concrete, or glass material used as a finish floor, wall, or ceiling covering. Tile comes in many different sizes, shapes, colors, and patterns.

tilt-up construction

A method of construction where walls will be cast on the ground or floor in a horizontal position and tilted up into position.

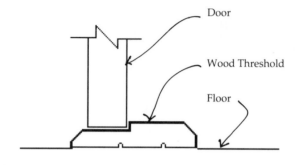

Door Sill

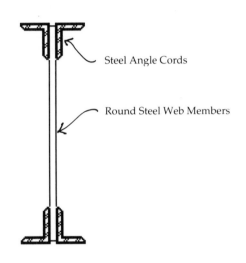

Steel Angle Cords

Round Steel Web Members

**Steel Truss (Bar Joist)
Cross Section**

timber

On plans and in specifications, the word "timber" applies to wood members whose dimensions exceed 4" x 6".

toenailing

This toenailing is the driving of a nail or brad in a slanted manner. It is most evident in laying tongue- and-groove wood floors.

tongue and groove

A joint made by two pieces of lumber with a corresponding tongue and groove.

toothing

In brickwork, toothing is allowing alternate courses of brick to project tooth like and fitting corresponding courses into the voids. Instructions in most specifications will prohibit toothing for fear that a full layer of mortar will not be obtainable at the top of the fitted brick.

topping

A thin layer of cement, sand, and water used to create a finished surface on concrete floors.

tracery

This is a term used to describe designs on glass panels or windows.

transom

A small window over a door or another window.

trim

On architectural drawings and in specifications, trim refers to the finishing woodwork on the exterior or interior of a building.

truss

A structural member made up of a combination of elements arranged in triangular units to form a rigid frame. Trusses come in a variety of designs, sizes, and materials.

Uniform Federal Accessibility Standards (UFAS)

Federal standards for providing access to handicapped users of buildings, sites, and structures.

valley

The depressed angle formed by the intersection at the bottom of two inclined sides of a roof.

vapor barrier

A material or construction designed to retard the passage of vapor through walls or ceilings.

vault

An arched structural form that forms a ceiling.

vellum

A 100 percent rag content paper used for drawings.

vent pipe

A pipe or flue designed to exhaust gases or fumes from building fixtures, such as a water closet, to a vent stack.

verge board

The board under the verge (edge) of a gable roof.

vermiculite

This is an expanded mica used as an aggregate in some concretes and plaster.

vestibule

On architectural plans, a vestibule is usually a small room used as an entrance to a building.

wainscot

A wall covering on the lower portion of an interior wall. Wainscoting may be wood, fabric, tile, or any other material.

water table

Dense material at the base of a building installed to prevent the migration of ground water (rising damp) up into the structure. On historic buildings this material may be stone, or a fired brick, and may project out from the plane of the building wall. In contemporary construction a traditional water table has been replaced by metal or rubber flashing.

weep hole

An opening through mortar joints in unit masonry walls, or through concrete retaining walls, to allow drainage of condensed moisture or ground water.

weld symbols

On structural drawings these are used to identify the type and size of welded connections between metal components.

winders

Stair treads used when stairs are circular, or are carried around curves or angles. Winders are wider at one end than the other.

wind loads

The pressure or force exerted on a structure by the wind. This will vary greatly, depending on the geographic location of the site.

window schedule

On architectural plans, a listing which identifies all windows in a building, providing location, type, size, operation, and finish.

withe (wythe)

In masonry construction, a single vertical wall of brick.

wood lath

A traditional material used on walls and ceilings as a base for plastering. Wood lath is made up of narrow strips of wood nailed to the wall framing.

working drawing

A finished drawing containing all necessary information to complete all, or a portion, of a project.

WWM (Welded Wire Mesh)

This is a type of metal reinforcing used primarily in concrete slabs to prevent tension cracking. It is manufactured in many different size patterns and weights. Notations on drawings will indicate the size and weight in numbers, such as 6 x 6 10/10 WWM. This represents a grid of wire mesh, 6" x 6", made of 10-gauge wire with welded joints. Depending on the type of application, the mesh could have larger or smaller squares and lighter or heavier wire. The mesh is placed about one inch down from the top of the slab, where the majority of tension stresses will occur.

wythe

See withe.

Steel Plates

Fillet Weld Symbol

Fillet Weld

Architectural Graphic Standards
Ramsey-Sleeper
New York: John Wiley & Sons, Inc., eighth edition, 1988

Building Construction Illustrated
by Francis D. K. Ching with Cassandra Adams
New York: VanNostrand Reinhold, 1974

Dictionary of Architecture and Construction
edited by Cyril M. Harris
New York: McGraw-Hill, second edition, 1993

Restoring Old Buildings for Contemporary Uses
by William Shopsin
New York: Whitney Library of Design, 1986

Sweet's Catalog File
New York: McGraw-Hill, 1993

Simplified Engineering for Architects and Builders
by Harry Parker
New York: John Wiley & Sons, Inc., 1991

Time-Saver Standards for Architectural Design Data
by John Hancock Callender
New York: McGraw-Hill, sixth edition, 1954

Time-Saver Standards for Landscape Architecture
by Charles W. Harris and Nicholas T. Dines
New York: McGraw-Hill, 1988

Time-Saver Standards for Site Planning
by Joseph DeChiara and Lee E. Koppelman
New York: McGraw-Hill, 1984

Traditional Details for Building Restoration, Renovation and Rehabilitation,
from the 1932-1951 Editions of Architectural Graphic Standards
New York: John Wiley & Sons, Inc., 1991

The following industry publications are issued on a periodic basis. The most current version of each should be sought.

MASTERSPEC®
American Institute of Architects
Washington, D. C.

BOCA Code
Homewood, Ill.: Building Officials & Code Administrators International, Inc.

Uniform Building Code (UBC)
Whittier, Calif.: International Congress of Building Officials

Southern Building Code (SBC)
Birmingham, Ala.: Southern Building Code Congress International, Inc.

National Building Code (NBC)
New York: Engineering and Safety Service

As a method of explaining the application of the Secretary of the Interior's Standards for Rehabilitation and Guidelines for Rehabilitating Historic Buildings, the National Park Service has issued a series of publications referred to as "Preservation Briefs." These documents focus on specific buildings systems, construction materials or methods. Currently there are 27 Preservation Briefs. A complete set of Preservation Briefs can be obtained through the Government Printing Office in Washington, D.C.

Preservation Brief #1: "The Cleaning and Waterproof Coating of Masonry Buildings"

Preservation Brief #2: "Repointing Mortar Joints in Historic Buildings"

Preservation Brief #3: "Conserving Energy in Historic Buildings"

Preservation Brief #4: "Roofing for Historic Buildings"

Preservation Brief #5: "Preservation of Adobe Buildings"

Preservation Brief #6: "Dangers of Abrasive Cleaning to Historic Buildings"

Preservation Brief #7: "The Preservation of Historic Glazed Terra-Cotta"

Preservation Brief #8: "Aluminum and Vinyl Siding on Historic Buildings"

Preservation Brief #9: "The Repair of Historic Wooden Windows"

Preservation Brief #10: "Exterior Paint Problems on Historic Woodwork"

Preservation Brief #11: "Rehabilitating Historic Storefronts"

Preservation Brief #12: "The Preservation of Historic Pigmented Structural Glass"

Preservation Brief #13: "The Repair and Thermal Upgrading of Historic Steel Windows"

Preservation Brief #14: "New Exterior Additions to Historic Buildings: Preservation Concerns"

Preservation Brief #15: "Preservation of Historic Concrete: Problems and General Approaches"

Preservation Brief #16: "The Use of Substitute Materials on Historic Building Exteriors"

Preservation Brief #17: "Architectural Character: Identifying the Visual Aspects of Historic Buildings as an Aid to Preserving Their Character"

Preservation Brief #18: "Rehabilitating Interiors in Historic Buildings"

Preservation Brief #19: "The Repair and Replacement of Wooden Shingle Roofs"

Preservation Brief #20: "The Preservation of Barns"

Preservation Brief #21: "The Repair of Historic Flat Plaster--Walls and Ceilings"

Preservation Brief #22: "The Preservation and Repair of Historic Stucco"

Preservation Brief #23: "Preserving Historic Ornamental Plaster"

Preservation Brief #24: "Heating, Ventilating, and Cooling Historic Buildings:Problems and Recommended Approaches"

Preservation Brief #25: "The Preservation of Historic Signs"

Preservation Brief #26: "The Preservation and Repair of Historic Log Buildings"

Preservation Brief #27: "The Maintenance and Repair of Architectural Cast Iron"

About the author

John Cullinane is the principal in the architectural and preservation planning firm of John Cullinane Associates in Washington, D.C. From 1976 until late last year, he served as senior architect for the (President's) Advisory Council on Historic Preservation in Washington. Prior to that he was executive director of the Preservation Alliance in Louisville, Kentucky, and practiced architecture in that city.